W9-BOL-019

Gridlock

GRIDLOCK

DOUBLEDAY

NEW YORK LONDON TORONTO

SYDNEY AUCKLAND

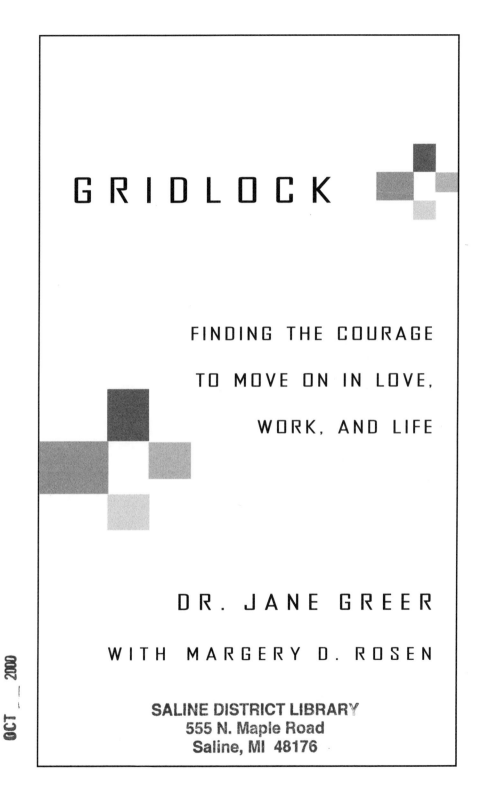

GRIDLOCK

FINDING THE COURAGE TO MOVE ON IN LOVE, WORK, AND LIFE

DR. JANE GREER

WITH MARGERY D. ROSEN

PUBLISHED BY DOUBLEDAY
a division of Random House, Inc.
1540 Broadway, New York, New York 10036

DOUBLEDAY and the portrayal of an anchor with a dolphin are
trademarks of Doubleday, a division of
Random House, Inc.

Book design by Dana Leigh Treglia

Library of Congress Cataloging-in-Publication Data

Greer, Jane, 1951–
    Gridlock: finding the courage to move on in love, work, and life / by Jane
    Greer with Margery D. Rosen.—1st ed.
        p. cm.
    Includes bibliographical references.
    1. Change (Psychology) 2. Change (Psychology)—Case studies.   I. Rosen,
    Margery D.   II. Title.
    BF637.C4 G74 2000
    158—dc21   99-053470
                                                                                CIP

Copyright © 2000 by Dr. Jane Greer & Margery D. Rosen
ISBN 0-385-49473-4

All Rights Reserved
Printed in the United States of America
May 2000
First Edition

10   9   8   7   6   5   4   3   2   1

In memory of
my beloved mother, Helen (with a liquid L),
who was always with me
and still is.

JANE

For my parents,
Irene and Lester David,
masters of words, who inspired and guided me.
I love you always.

MARGERY

ACKNOWLEDGMENTS

As a psychotherapist, I consider it my first priority to safeguard the confidentiality of my patients and interview subjects. In the interest of protecting their privacy, I have changed the names of all persons mentioned in the book, except the psychologists and other theorists quoted. I have also altered the details of people's lives—their professions, family specifics, and other potentially identifying circumstances.

I first want to express my appreciation and gratitude to all the people I work with who have shared their gridlock experiences with me and have mustered the courage to move on.

I also want to thank . . .

Margery D. Rosen, my writing partner and friend, who consistently challenged me to take the high road in order to write the best book possible.

My agents, Pam Bernstein and Donna Downing, of Pam Bernstein Associates, for their faith in the project and their never-ending spirit and support.

Debbie Cowell, my editor, for your wonderful enthusiasm, interest, and receptivity, which lifted this project off the ground.

Dr. Josie Palleja, my cherished friend, official "sister," and colleague; your theoretical collaboration and refueling were worth their weight in gold. Thank you for your limitless love and wisdom, and for sharing every facet of my life with your grace and finesse.

Kathy Pomerantz, treasured pal of mine. Throughout all the years, you have never let me down. Thank you for your laughter, love, and vitality, which are a part of my heart.

Louise DuArt, my dearest buddy and Celebrity Solutions partner. Thank you for your warm heart, delightful witty ways, and for bringing wonderful happenings into my life.

Lesley Krupnik, for remaining an angel in my life.

Immeasurable thanks to: Charles and Peggy Cook, Maria Pappapetros, Sara and Vic Carlson, Judith Newman, Sally Kravich, Dr. Sonya Rhodes, and Cynthia Richmond. Your friendship, light, energy, love, and support sustain me with peace of heart and serenity of mind.

I thank my family—my father, brother, Aunt Ruth, and cousins—for their ever-present love. Also my in-laws: the Snowmans and the Aprils. Most especially, I thank my amazing husband and colleague, Marc Snowman. Each day you fill my heart with tenderness and nurture my soul with your continuous flow of love and understanding. You make it all worthwhile.

—DR. JANE GREER

A million thanks to Jane Greer, my incredibly optimistic, indefatigable writing partner, who never seems to have a bad day and has taught me how to see that the glass really is half full. Writing this and other books with you is more fun than work.

To Pam Bernstein and Donna Downing, my gratitude for your astute perceptions, insight, perseverence, and belief in this idea from the start.

To Debbie Cowell, our bright, energetic editor, thank you for your enthusiasm from the get-go and your invaluable advice.

To all my friends, and you know who you are, who have not only shared your stories for this book but shared your lives with me. Knowing you're there makes all the difference, and I'm deeply grateful.

To my wonderful husband, Baran, and my two terrific children, Sarah and Michael, who have always been my greatest cheerleaders and strongest supporters, not to mention fodder for innumerable anecdotes. I thank you for being you, and I love you with all my heart.

—MARGERY D. ROSEN

CONTENTS

GRIDLOCK

PART ONE

ARE YOU STUCK?

CHAPTER ONE

HOW TO SPOT A

DEAD-END RELATIONSHIP

Danielle, a public-relations executive whose client roster reads like a Who's Who in film, politics, and media, seems to have it all. Dressed in a black sheath and Sabrina-heel shoes, her pale-blue pashmina shawl casually wrapped around her toned shoulders, she sank into the couch in my office with a deep sigh. "I'm thirty-four, I manage a bicoastal PR agency, I've already made more money than my parents ever did—and I'm miserable," she said, her steady voice belying a barely concealed anxiety I've come to recognize in many young women these days. "I've exceeded my dreams," Danielle continued. "For the past ten years I've poured every ounce of energy into my work. I've loved it, and I'm very proud of what I've accomplished. Not to mention the fact that it's extremely glamorous to fly first class, eat at fancy restaurants, and hobnob with people whose names appear in boldface in the gossip columns.

But though I've worked hard to get here, the truth is, I'm burned out. And lonely. I'm dating two men—if you can call it that. I hardly see either of them because of work conflicts. And there's been no one special in my life for years. Considering my hours, how could there be? I can't find time to take care of a dog, let alone a relationship. But I'd be lying if I said I loved being single. I want a meaningful relationship with someone who thinks I'm special. I want to be married. I want a child. Yet I feel trapped, and it's all my own fault. Some days I think about quitting, even though the very idea is terrifying. How would I support myself? But if I don't, I'm heading toward a goal that no longer holds any meaning for me. Does this make any sense? I always thought this was what I wanted to do with my life, but now I'm not sure. I don't know what to do, and I feel so stuck. Am I expecting too much?"

Like many of her contemporaries, independent, spunky Danielle has earned an impressive reputation and a résumé to match. But on a personal level, she's nowhere near where she wants to be. The pride she justifiably derives from her accomplishments is tinged with anxiety; the joy of reaching a goal, shadowed by the loneliness of crawling into bed each night alone. Depressed and confused, she doesn't know what to do or where to turn to relieve her pain. "This is one problem I just can't fix," she said sadly. And so the woman who seems to have it all stays stuck.

She's hit gridlock.

At one time or another, you probably have, too. Although the people or situations may change, gridlock's impact remains strikingly the same: You are not getting what you want and need in love, in work, or in life—and chances are you never will. You are stalled in a relationship or a situation that is empty, unfulfilling, or hurtful. Yet, for reasons you can't fully understand, you hang on and continue to rationalize what you are doing and why you are staying in a dead-end situation that is clearly toxic to your emotional and physical well-being.

Gridlock is the inertia that keeps you stuck. It is all those experiences trapped in your unconscious mind that are replicated over and over again in each relationship you have and each life choice you make. When you're gridlocked, you feel angry, edgy, or frustrated, yet you're unable to put your finger on why a particular person, work situation, or life choice is so damaging to your self-confidence and self-esteem. You are giving too much to, and getting too little back from, people who seem unavailable and unsupportive. You feel defeated, hopeless, and above all, trapped in a position that is clearly unyielding—but you have no idea how to move on. Moreover, you're not entirely convinced that you should. You inhabit an emotional wasteland. Your head tells you one thing, your heart another.

WHAT KEEPS YOU STUCK?

If you're reading this book, you're probably hungry for more passion, enthusiasm, challenge, and stimulation in some area of your life—and you'd like to think you're flexible and responsive enough to find it. You've always assumed that at least in some ways you're the master of your own fate. But sometimes attaining such a seemingly simple goal means relinquishing all that is secure—and that can be a terrifying prospect. Each step forward may entail a step away from the familiar into the confusing nowhere of in-betweenness.

One reason is the dual nature of change itself: It can fill us with a sense of excitement, the promise of something new, and the deep satisfaction of having met a challenge we thought unattainable. But it can also flood us with dread. Letting go when you don't know what lies around the corner, coupled with fear of the struggle you must go through to get there, can be overwhelming. Taking a chance on change means putting your emotional security at risk—an often immobilizing proposition. Even positive change—a job promotion, a new baby, a move to a larger apartment in a nicer neighborhood, getting married, winning an award or competition—can trigger anxiety that you will be unable to meet your own, and everyone else's, expectations.

Then, too, each new beginning involves a loss of some kind. Ending a marriage or a friendship, saying good-bye to a person or situation always entails relinquishing the sense of control or the feeling of being loved and supported that the person or situation provided for you. You may be thrilled to be pregnant for the first time but sad, worried, and angry at your new baby's intrusion into your life and your inability to find half an hour alone with your husband. Even something seemingly silly can provoke the same feelings of unsureness: Dana, a thirty-two-year-old buyer for a department store, recalled how unsettled she'd felt during the first few weeks at her new job in a new city: "I'd worked at my old company since I'd graduated from college, and I was really psyched to move on. But for the longest time I couldn't get my bearings. My routines were off, and everything was so unfamiliar. I hadn't realized how much I had counted on the small stuff to give me a sense of solidity: The guy at the deli who knew just how I liked my coffee and corn muffin . . . the checkout girl at the supermarket who'd cash a check for me when I ran short and the banks were closed. I'd moved into my work mode far more easily than it took to rebuild those outside connections."

Of course, another reason you may stay gridlocked is your temperament, those innate characteristics that influence how you deal with the world. Some fearless adventurers naturally welcome change and handle it well. They relish the unexpected and the risky, even seek it out, while others have always been, and to some extent will remain, inhibited and cautious. Your temperament, shaped by key developmental experiences in your childhood, forms your Gridlock Quotient, or GQ, which I'll discuss in the next chapter. Your GQ is a critical factor that affects your ability to focus on what you really want and make it happen. But first let's take a closer look at where and how you may be stuck.

TIES THAT BIND

Sometimes the ties that keep you gridlocked are obvious. Perhaps you are long married and have children to consider, not to mention your financial security. Perhaps you work with, or for, an overbearing, controlling boss, yet to leave a job you love or need simply to erase this person from your life seems like cutting off your nose to spite your face. Or perhaps you've unwittingly slid into a personal comfort zone: You're busy and . . . well, content—but definitely not happy and definitely not where you really want to be.

But more often the ties that keep you stuck are like a spider web, invisible unless you know where to look. You may, for example, be staying in a dead-end relationship out of guilt. Many women feel it's somehow better to suffer the hurt and humiliation of a poisonous friendship because they don't want to hurt someone's feelings. That's what Marlena, an assistant professor of economics at a small New England college, did for sixteen years until she finally had the courage to end a toxic friendship with college roommate Karen. "We all knew that Karen was a bit of a know-it-all," Marlena admitted, "but she could also be tons of fun. I managed somehow to overlook the negative, and much to everyone else's astonishment, we became very close. Though we went our separate ways after graduation—she got married and quit the law firm she was working for to be a suburban mom; I stayed single and moved into academia—we stayed in touch by phone and had lunch every few months. Karen knew me inside and out, and there was a big comfort factor in that. I liked having someone who could remember how bummed out it felt to be the only two on campus without a date for homecoming weekend. But I always ended a visit with her feeling depleted in some way. No matter how much I tried, every conversation fell into the same pattern of me asking for advice and Karen dispensing it, usually in a voice tinged with condescension. I'd listen, and sometimes agree with her, but her suggestions never made me feel good. If I told her I was going to apply for a promotion or a new grant, she'd say, 'Well, Marlena, it sounds good, but you know how you handle pressure,' or 'I wouldn't count on it; I hear grant money is tight these days.' Still, we'd been friends forever. Besides, for a long time I couldn't put my finger on what was bothering me, so I never told her how I was feeling. But if I ever questioned her advice or failed to follow her suggestions, I sensed I was hurting her personally."

It wasn't until Marlena was faced with one of the toughest dilemmas of her life that she finally heard the message that others, as well as her own intuition, had been broadcasting for years. During a three-day conference retreat, the head of her department propositioned her. The day after Marlena turned him down, she awoke to discover that he'd begun to spread malicious rumors about her, questioning her professional decisions and personal standards. A few months later she was denied a promotion she and everyone else knew she deserved. "I was seriously contemplating a sexual-harassment suit, and since Karen was a lawyer, I naturally called her to discuss it. I was shocked at how unsupportive she was. 'You don't know what you're up against,' she warned. 'What makes you think you'll win? You'll waste a lot of time and money. Then where will you be?' This time I heard the archness in her voice. She sounded like a scolding, I-told-you-so mother, not a responsive, helpful friend. I felt abandoned by her. I hung up the phone and never called or returned her calls again. That's when it dawned on me that Karen had never cared about what was truly important to me. She didn't care about what was best for *me*, but what *she* thought was best for me."

Marlena had striven to make an untenable situation work until she eventually snuffed out her own true feelings and needs. No wonder she didn't have any faith in her own decisions. Others may be so desperate for approval or fearful of being alone that they endlessly tolerate feeling rejected and deprived, hooked on the promise of change that another person offers. The partner of an alcoholic who swears he'll quit drinking but keeps falling off the wagon, the spouse of a gambler who insists he will never place another bet but always does, or the wife of an adulterer who swears he'll be the man you always thought he'd be but winds up in the arms of another on his next business trip—all face repeated instances of broken trust. As a result, they don't know when to trust their own judgment or whether a partner's promise today is real or merely lip service. They stay gridlocked, hoping, expecting, believing that someday soon things will change. But they never do.

Sometimes you stay stuck because it's hard to go against the flow of what others expect of you. Maybe it's being a stay-at-home mom because your husband doesn't want anyone else raising your children, though you can't wait to get back in the workforce. Or maybe it's holding on to a job you don't really like for the benefits it provides. "About two years ago I realized that my job just wasn't challenging anymore, and that's when I first toyed with the idea of moving to Los Angeles," recalled Leslie, who reads and develops scripts for a film company. "I felt like a machine every day. I'd done, and learned, all I could, and there wasn't much room for creativity. But it wasn't a horrible situation either. I didn't hate my colleagues or have an ogre of a boss. I was just bored. It seemed that at twenty-seven I was going through a midlife crisis. My gut instinct told me to make this move, but my friends and family thought I was crazy. 'How can you move across the country to a strange city where you have no job and know no one?' they kept asking. So for two years I stayed, and sank deeper and deeper in this rut. The idea of moving *was* scary. I knew it was a risk, but I also firmly believe that if nothing's ventured, nothing's gained. I finally decided it was time to start a new chapter in my life, and the only way to do it was to leave New York and try living in L.A."

As Leslie discovered, even a change for the better can evoke feelings of guilt that may make you second-guess your decisions. That's because gridlock can actually trigger stressful, anxious, self-doubting feelings that may seem similar to the bad situation itself. What's more, when you're swamped by self-doubts, you may convince yourself—wrongly—that you simply don't have what it takes to make a change.

That's what kept Monica gridlocked. After three years as executive assistant to a producer at a cable channel, Monica felt "emotionally burned out. There was no special crisis, no one thing that made me feel this way," she said. "I'd even gotten a great performance review, but I still didn't feel I was doing a good job. I was miserable, but I reported for work and operated on automatic pilot. I couldn't get excited about anything, yet I couldn't tell you one thing was really wrong either." In time, people like Monica lose faith in themselves, their judgment and abilities. Even if they are aware of their problem, they may be so demoralized and resigned that they stay stuck instead of harnessing the courage within them to move on.

And finally you may become gridlocked because in some way you are re-creating in a relationship or situation many of the issues and problems you had in your family of origin. For example, if you grew up feeling unloved and unworthy, unconsciously you may enter into lopsided friendships or make unsatisfactory life choices. After all, that's how you first experienced love and intimacy, so it becomes the way you expect others to treat you. Tina, thirty-four, a market researcher, the mother of a three-year-old daughter and an eight-year-old son, has always been the person others turn to in a crisis. "I spend more time ministering to my friends' emotional upheavals than I do to my own," Tina said, sighing. "I can't say no. If someone needs to talk, I listen. If someone asks for a small loan, I give. If two dozen cupcakes are needed for the Halloween party at school, I always bake them, even if it's at two-thirty in the morning. If my son wants to have four friends sleep over on the night before I have to be somewhere bright and early the next day, I say okay. Part of the time I feel like a complete jerk. And part of the time I feel like I really should do these things, that I'm not a good person, or a good mother, unless I do."

I soon learned where Tina's feelings came from: Her father had died suddenly when she was only fifteen, and Tina, the older of two daughters, was thrust into the role of caring for her ten-year-old sister as well as her grieving mother, who fell into a deep depression when her husband died. Tina felt valued only for what she did, rather than for who she was. She felt loved only when she was doing for, or giving to, others. Deep down Tina is still so desperate to feel valued and loved that she's become everybody's doormat. Though she's beginning to realize how stuck she is, she still can't change.

The same invisible ties keep Barbara stuck in a morass of indecision and unhappiness. By anyone's standards, Barbara, thirty-nine, is an astonishing success. The mother of three school-age children in a Boston suburb, she's editorial director of a small publishing company, where she uses her background in art history and decorative arts to oversee a variety of projects. Barbara also sells antique furniture, clothes, and jewelry, but only to longtime clients—people she worked with before she had children, when she managed a prestigious gallery on Newbury Street.

"Even as a kid I was always doing three or four things at a time," explained Barbara, the older of two sisters, her words tumbling out in rapid fire as she leans forward in her chair to make her point. "My mother was like that, too. She painted, made pottery, and sold jewelry. But while other people seem amazed that I do all this, I don't feel particularly good about it. It's hard to explain—I don't mean to sound ungrateful, or like I'm fishing for compliments. I honestly don't feel satisfied or accomplished or even particularly happy. Every step of the way I feel anxious and unfulfilled. People tell me I'm doing a good job at work, but I don't think I am. It's as if this dark cloud of insecurity shadows me wherever I go.

"Each time I commit to a project," Barbara continued, "I'll be excited at first. But before long the thrill wanes and all these doubts rise up and grab me by the throat. I start to think, 'Is this really what I want to be doing? Does this fully utilize all my talents?' There's a piece missing from my life—and I don't know where to look for it."

Barbara had that piece once—right after college, when she worked for a struggling dance company in Cambridge. "I did everything from scrounging for props and making coffee to actually choreographing," Barbara recalled. "I was never happier. Of course, I was barely able to support myself, but the thrill of being on the ground floor of something so exciting with all these dedicated people made it totally worthwhile."

But soon Barbara fell in love, married, and started a family, choices she gladly made and definitely doesn't regret. "Continuing with the dance company didn't make sense then. I'd do anything to get back to it, but now's just not the right time. Besides, I've been out of the business for so long, how can I possibly get back in? If I called my old theater colleagues, they'd laugh at me. But the truth is, nothing I've done since then has ever held the same passion for me."

In the next chapter I'll zero in on why people like Barbara become gridlocked by old childhood roles that carry over into their adult lives. For now, let's examine the specific circumstances that keep us gridlocked.

ROADBLOCKS TO MOVING ON

In my practice I often work with successful people who voice profound disappointment and disillusionment about the quality of their lives and their apparent inability to make them better. Over and over again they describe a vague but pervasive sense of being unhappy and stuck. Passive and immobilized, they wait at a stoplight for some signal that they can move on—but the light never changes. The physical symptoms these people describe seem random to them, yet they're remarkably similar: They're exhausted and stressed; they may even have lost interest in the people or things that used to bring them pleasure. Many are bewildered that they can be so assertive, productive, and successful in some areas of their lives and so paralyzed in others. Eventually they downshift to accepting their unhappiness as part of the status quo.

Many are stuck in what I call **Here-and-Now Roadblocks,** the immediate problems or crises with which you know you must deal but somehow don't or won't. You can't bring yourself to schedule an appointment for a mammogram even though your doctor, and every magazine and newspaper article you read, advises that women over forty should have one annually. Or perhaps the company for whom you work is downsizing, but you still haven't updated your résumé, and the thought of making a few phone calls to begin the networking process gives you laryngitis. That's the kind of roadblock that gridlocked Ray, thirty-nine, a vice president of corporate finance at a major Wall Street brokerage house. Ray knew that his company, like many others on the Street, was floundering in the wake of a recession and stock-market downturn. Yet he ignored rumors of companywide cutbacks, insisting he didn't know where he'd find a job that filled his needs as well as his current one did and reassuring himself that he was safe since his immediate supervisor was one of the sons of the founding partners. "Besides," he kept saying, "right now, there are a million guys out there looking for the same job I'm looking for. I'll wait and see what happens." When his division was consolidated with another, Ray's connections couldn't help him, and he was unemployed for seven months.

Here-and-Now Roadblocks have some urgency to them, but they are often surrounded by a wall of fear. How you chip away at that fear in spite of the crisis you may be facing can make the difference between attaining an effective and independent way of coping that affords you the attention, support, and resources you need and remaining gridlocked in a helpless, dependent mode.

Of course, sometimes Here-and-Now Roadblocks seem to resolve themselves simply with the passage of time. That's what happened to Shawna, a teacher who worked part-time in her daughter's elementary school and was offered a full-time position when one of the women took maternity leave and decided she didn't want to return to work. Shawna wanted the job—she loved working with children, knew her family could use the steady income, and felt hampered by her inability to see the children on a regular, full-time basis—but she waffled for several weeks trying to figure out if it was worth giving up the freedom she had as a substitute. By the time she finally decided to go for it, the job had already been filled, and she felt more stuck than ever. However, had she taken the initiative, she would have had a say in the resolution of her dilemma and in the end would have felt more capable and self-sufficient. And she'd have the tools to get herself unstuck each time she hit another Here-and-Now Roadblock.

Then there are the **Transitional Roadblocks,** those that can be linked to the inevitable milestones or turning points in life that demand decisions you are unable to make, changes you don't feel ready for but believe you should have made by now. Perhaps you worked hard for two years to get your M.B.A. but have no clue what kind of job to pursue. Perhaps you've been dating the person of your dreams for three years but can't commit to a wedding date. Or perhaps you've been married for years, invited to countless baby showers, and still can't decide if you're mommy material. Marriage, childbirth, illness, retirement, a milestone birthday, starting over after divorce or the death of a spouse, the empty nest when kids leave home for college—these are the life transitions that can trigger the anxiety, guilt, or anger that leads to gridlock. A Transitional Roadblock crops up while you're still going forward. The trouble is, to reach your goal you really should be taking a different highway.

Hillary is gridlocked at a Transitional Roadblock. At forty-four, with two children, fourteen and eleven, she can no longer justify her stay-at-home-mom status on a full-time basis yet can't make up her mind about returning to work as an elementary-school teacher, a job she quit when her first child was born. "I really want to work. We could certainly use the money, and with the kids away until dinnertime most days, I'm bored. I hated being a teacher, though, but that's really all I'm trained to do. I don't have the experience for anything else. I'd have to go back for additional training, but who can sit in a classroom and take notes and study for exams after all this time? I did call two colleges to get their brochures, but when I saw that most of the courses I need to take are given at night . . . well, how could I manage that with the kids? That's when they're home and need me for homework help and to monitor all the evening craziness."

People like Hillary can't figure out how and where to start. Even continuing with life choices they've already made can feel like traveling on a strange new road, since they no longer have a clear vision of what comes next. Those trapped in Transitional Roadblocks know what they *don't* want but not what they do want, so they sidestep all decision-making. As a result, they may become a passive observer of their own lives, allowing time, or someone else, to do the changing for them.

And finally there are the **Long-standing Roadblocks,** those triggered by doubts you had all along but ignored. Feeling pressured and overpowered, you may have struck out in one direction because you didn't feel then, and don't now, that you had any other real options. Perhaps you sensed early on that you and your mate were not compatible, but got married anyway, and fifteen years and three kids later, you're still unhappy but unable to end the relationship. Or maybe you've held the same position in your company for so long you can do the job in your sleep, but you garner little joy and even less personal satisfaction from your accomplishments. Whereas people stuck in Transitional Roadblocks are unable to identify the choices available to them, those gridlocked at Long-standing Roadblocks can see their options, but each one seems untenable. Hopeless, they resign themselves for years to an unfulfilling job or marriage.

Long-standing Roadblocks are sometimes precipitated by a previous betrayal or setback. Jay, thirty-nine, was gridlocked in his job as a top administrator in a large bank. "I've been here for eight years and I know I'm doing a good job, but I'm unhappy," Jay told me. "In a funny way, though, I don't feel I have the right to be. I was fired from my last job, and I'm scared to make a change. The firing was my fault. I was fresh out of business school and very naïve. I didn't know how the system worked, and I didn't generate enough ideas or take enough initiative on my own. When they asked me to leave, I was devastated. After pounding the pavement for five months, I swore I'd never make the same mistakes. And I've done everything right, moving up until I now administer a fifteen-person department. The trouble is, I dislike being the boss, and I'm not thrilled with banking anymore. But I have a family to support. How can I explore other job options that won't pay the same?"

Similarly, if you've been the victim of betrayal, particularly in a love relationship, you may be so untrusting of your own judgment and feel so undeserving of very much from a partner that you retreat to whoever feels safe, no matter how unsatisfying that relationship may be. You may jump into a rebound romance with someone you don't really love but who seems to offer shelter in a storm.

YOUR STUCK STYLE

In addition to being stuck behind the situational roadblocks that test your resources and capacity for effecting change, you also deal with change through learned patterns of behavior. While you may recognize that these patterns are hurtful and unproductive, they are nevertheless comfortable. You slide into them easily, like old shoes that don't quite fit but have worn calluses on your feet. Rarely do you find the courage to say, "This relationship isn't working" ... "This job is going nowhere" ... "I made a poor choice—so I'm ending it and making a new and better one."

In fact, these patterns of decision-making and handling change—

what I call your Stuck Style—are deeply ingrained. They influence not only why you become gridlocked but also the way in which you grind yourself into a rut. What's more, though the choices and changes you may contemplate in life will be different, your Stuck Style—that is, your coping response to the external stress and internal distress that change of any kind dredges up—stays remarkably the same, thanks to the powerful combination of temperament and life experiences layered one on top of the other. However, once you acquire some insight as well as more effective skills and techniques for managing change, you'll get stuck less often and get out of a rut more quickly. This book will be a first step.

As you'll see, each of the four most common Stuck Styles outlined below is linked with key feelings that hark back to infancy and toddlerhood, when you first began exploring the world as a separate, independent person. In Chapter 2 we'll uncover the origins of the Stuck Styles. But first let's take a closer look at the four most common ones.

STANDSTILLS: These procrastinators are able to go only partway to reach their goal before they're forced to stop and wait—helpless and anxious—for someone or something to change so they can get moving again. Afraid to venture forth on their own—often the mere thought of exploration and checking things out overwhelms them—they wind up in a dependent relationship with a boyfriend or girlfriend, spouse, parent, or boss.

Standstills are often passengers in their own life. They need to be driven and believe they have no control over where they're headed. Nor do they feel equipped in any way to get there. Blaming themselves for their lack of initiative, they think they're stupid, incompetent, or lazy. Of course, such negative self-talk only perpetuates their inertia. Do you know a guy with cold feet who just can't commit to marriage? He's a Standstill. He's so afraid of intimacy that he'll allow himself to go just so far in a relationship. The brilliant accountant who can't bring himself to take the exam he needs to move up in his firm? He's a Standstill, too. On some level Standstills suffer from a fear of success. After all, success equals independence, and the anxiety attached to it stops them cold.

Alana is a typical Standstill. "I finally do realize it's not the men I'm dating, it's me," admitted Alana, thirty, a newspaper reporter who has been in therapy before. "There's just something holding me back, and it probably has to do with the fact that my parents were divorced when I was nine and I hardly ever saw my dad. He remarried, started a new family, and lost contact with me. But that little bit of insight doesn't seem to help me. I never change. I'll meet a great guy, date him for five or six months, but always, just when he's beginning to get serious, I find something wrong. It finally dawned on me that this wasn't some kind of slump I was in. It was a lifestyle." Since her father never showed any real interest in her over the years, it's hard for her to trust that any man will, because to do so would leave her open and vulnerable. Paradoxically, Alana leaves them before they leave her. And though she's aware of the pattern, she's so gridlocked she can't break out. Alana knows it's not easy to forge a healthy relationship, but she often gives up before she really tries.

U-TURNERS: These people try very hard to get unstuck—but they go about it in the wrong way. By moving too precipitously and impulsively, they lack the information they need to make a well-thought-out decision. Without a clear vision in sight, and before they've had time to research and weigh their options, they may panic, feel guilty, and quickly turn around. They may know that they're lost, but they refuse to ask directions; after all, such information would enable them to go forward. Instead they remain mired in frustration or retreat. Like Standstills, U-Turners need constant support, advice, and reassurance. In fact, without others to sustain them, they're easily depleted and soon run out of gas. U-Turners are often gridlocked in unhappy relationships. And though they may make repeated efforts to break up, their anxiety forces them back. To them, leaving signifies that they failed—or, worse yet, that no one else wants them. Melanie, twenty-eight, a manager for a Web site, fell head over heels in love with Richie, a documentary filmmaker, and has been dating him for three years, despite his playboy tendencies and despite his promises, never kept, to set a wedding date. Every few months, almost like clockwork, she tells him she doesn't want to see him anymore and starts dating someone else, only to be wooed back by his vows to reform and his insistence that he can't live without her. "I'm such a sucker, I know it, but I can't seem to do anything about it," she announced. "When he tells me how much he needs me, that without me in his life it's empty, I melt. Last year I even canceled vacation plans with a friend to go to Hawaii—and lost a ton of money—to spend the holidays with Richie. But as soon as I'm back on the scene, he goes right back to his old ways of taking me for granted, working late, and leaving me stranded in restaurants because he forgot we had plans." U-Turners like Melanie are so fearful of being on their own, and so dependent on someone else for love and approval, that they sacrifice and compromise their own well-being to keep another person in their life.

ENGINE FLOODERS: Whenever these people try to change, they immediately become swamped by angry feelings or embroiled in power struggles that hold them back or leave them depressed and depleted. Resentful of the situation they're in, they blame others and refuse to budge: "*I'm* not crazy—*she's* crazy," they'll gripe, or "It's not *my* problem, it's *her* problem—so why should I have to change?" They fully expect everyone else just to get out of their way and stop holding them back. Though Engine Flooders may feel guilty about what they want to do, they use their anger to justify their right to do it anyway. As one angry wife shouted to her husband, "Look, I really don't want to listen to your suggestions about discipline. You've been out of town for four days, you have no idea what I've been going through with these kids, so please keep your comments to yourself!"

As her husband learned, it can be a risky business to step in and offer a suggestion to Engine Flooders. They will inevitably counter with negativity and more anger, which further floods instead of fuels them. The same problems are brewing between Tom and Val, who have been married only two years. Tom, a surgeon, has been unable to sever his ties to his first wife, Harriet, the mother of his ten-year-old daughter, Jessica. "Harriet is driving me crazy, and that's causing big problems between me and Val," admitted Tom. "Harriet is lazy and disorganized, and I'm deeply concerned about how she's raising our daughter. I can already see some of those tendencies in Jessica. When Harriet calls—usually to whine or complain, I might add—I can never get off the phone with her. And she frequently makes it impossible for me to see Jessica. If Val and I plan a special weekend activity for the three of us—maybe get tickets to a show or ball game—at the last minute Harriet will come up with some reason that Jessica can't go with us. I've tried everything I can think of to get her to be more understanding and cooperative, but nothing works. Even a brief conversation with that woman leaves me fuming." To make matters worse, whenever Val tries to help Tom calm down and suggests ways to talk to Harriet, Tom turns his fury on her. Like all Engine Flooders, Tom is gridlocked in a situation he feels powerless to change and doesn't realize that as long as his guilt and anger keep him stuck in the past, he's sabotaging his present and his future.

FORKED ROADERS: No wonder they're gridlocked: Ambivalence drives them, and they can't figure out which way to go. Torn between two choices, they waver and ultimately go nowhere and do nothing. Or they call a halt to their journey out of fear that they may make an unalterable mistake and will be unable to get back on the right road. In this way they can continue to hold on to what they have, no matter how unfulfilling it may be.

In one sense, Forked Roaders want to have their cake and eat it, too. They're unable to accept the fact that often compromise or trade-off is a fact of life. People who have extramarital affairs are usually Forked Roaders, mired in two relationships, unable to choose. But still others are simply so overwhelmed by simple choices, they make none at all.

Forty-three-year-old Sarah, the mother of three children, aged fourteen, eleven, and nine, has been trying to decide since her youngest was born whether to look for a new apartment—a costly proposition—or renovate her current one to better suit her family's needs. Over the last few years she's spent thousands of dollars on architectural drawings to reconfigure her current space, as well as countless hours looking at apartments for sale. Yet she can't make up her mind whether to stay or to leave. "I really love our building and neighborhood, and moving will cost us a small fortune," she explained. "But I know that to do the kind of renovation I want will cost a small fortune, too—and even then, will I really get the space for a family room that I need? You know, it really makes no sense even to think about this right now. In a few months my husband will find out what his year-end bonus is; I should really wait until then. Besides, the market is at an all-time high right now. I know prices will come down after the new year." Always, Sarah has a perfectly logical reason for not making a move. Always, she stays stuck. She needs to learn how to balance the good with the bad, the pros with the cons, and then concentrate on the positive factors that a change will bring instead of allowing the negatives to drag her back.

Here's the paradox: When you're gridlocked in any way, you are, at least for the moment, safe. You may even be lulled into believing that your failure to make a decisive move was actually a good thing. "Everything worked out anyway," Sarah announced. "The one apartment I thought was perfect for us was snapped up the same day I saw it. But I wasn't really ready to move yet. Maybe by next year I'll have a better fix on what I really want and how much we can afford." But the truth is, when you fail to play an active role in your own life, the problems don't go away; they go underground and inevitably crop up later. "Right now I'm so confused about which camp to send my son to this summer, I can't think about moving," Sarah continued, oblivious to the pattern of her life. "I've got to figure that out. So far we've watched nine videos, and they all look great. I just can't make up my mind." While Forked Roaders like Sarah may be temporarily off the hook in one area, they're destined to become gridlocked at another time or in another way, regretting the decisions they didn't make or the opportunities lost in the process. The first step in making sure this doesn't happen is to take a closer look at how and why you may become gridlocked in the first place.

CHAPTER TWO

EMOTIONAL ROADBLOCKS

How the Past Holds You Back

Many of us are more afraid of a new pleasure than an old pain. Time and again we find it easier to remain gridlocked, plodding through one uneventful day after another or puddle-jumping from one crisis to the next, simply because doing so feels familiar. Paradoxically, any disruption to the status quo—even one that allows us to live our life the way we want to—can be unsettling, even terrifying. And most of us don't understand why. That's because we don't realize how profoundly our early-childhood relationships and experiences shape our personality.

Often, people ask me, "How can what happened so long ago still be affecting me now?" Or "All right, so it happened. I got over it. It's not something I even think about anymore. Why is it still such a big deal?" "Besides," everyone adds, "if I can't go back and change the past, what difference does it make?" The truth is, many of the difficulties you encounter in adulthood are really a continuation of the struggles around dependence, independence, and identity that began with your earliest efforts to separate from your parent or caregiver and form your own sense of who you are. As a result, you may still be operating with the same feelings of helplessness you had back then, without the tools that would enable you to cope more effectively.

Before you can even begin to effect real and lasting change in your life now, you have to find out why change is inherently so paralyzing for you. When you do, your attitude and perspective on change will shift. You'll be able to look upon the process as an opportunity to grow, the first step in developing the coping skills you might not have had the chance to develop years ago. Once you can identify your feelings, manage your fears so they don't hold you back, and confidently make decisions, you'll understand why you stay stuck or persist in using unworkable strategies to try to make a bad relationship or situation good. You'll finally break out of gridlock.

THE MYSTERIOUS LEGACIES
OF CHILDHOOD

How, exactly, does a child develop the ability to handle change in a positive way? What does he need to become an adult who feels worthy, competent, and confident of his decisions as well as his accomplishments? How does he develop the capacity to make and sustain healthy relationships, the strength to persevere in the face of adversity, or the resiliency to bounce back after failure? Ever since Freud first concluded that the ills of adulthood can be traced to those first few years of childhood, physicians, scientists, psychologists, and child-development experts in all disciplines have weighed in on the role of heredity, environment, peer relationships, and, of course, parenting on a child's emotional, intellectual, and psychological life. Each development theory, in turn, has been the subject of heated, often angry debate, defended and denounced endlessly as one study after another purports to undo what another previously extolled.

Still, over the years it's been generally accepted that early-childhood relationships and experiences form at least part of the blueprint for how we behave and relate to others, as well as how we expect others will treat us. We acknowledge, too, that the way in which a mother[1] responds to a child during the first few years of life actually shapes the skills and behaviors he needs to manage feelings of anxiety, fear, guilt, and anger later on. What's more, as I'll explain later in this chapter, these early struggles with parents often reappear in the way we relate to others as adults—be they spouses, friends, colleagues—or even in the way we parent our own children.

The work of three theorists is particularly helpful in understanding these critical connections. The late British researcher John Bowlby and the Canadian psychologist Mary Ainsworth, working around midcentury, first developed what they called the Attachment Theory, which focused on how freely a child could tolerate being alone to explore his world and still feel safe and secure when Mother wasn't around. If he missed her, the researchers wondered, how quickly could he be comforted upon her return? The key to achieving "secure attachment," the theory goes, is a parent who is sensitive, attentive, and nurturing. On the other hand, children who are "insecurely attached"—that is, who never received warm, supportive parenting—grow up with low self-esteem and often struggle to maintain secure, loving, trusting relationships. As children, they aren't able to be comforted, because they reject in anger Mom's attempts to soothe them. As adults, they are unable to express what they truly need and want. They may cling to people or situations that are wrong for them or angrily reject any help that is offered.

By the late 1970s the work of the well-respected psychoanalyst Margaret Mahler took Attachment Theory a step further. Mahler studied pairs of infants and mothers to form her theory of Separation and Individuation, and it remains one of the benchmarks for tracking a child's emotional, social, and psychological growth. Her research offered the first empirical evidence that some psychological problems had their roots in childhood. She also laid the groundwork for our understanding of how early development may predict the quality of a person's emotional life, not just at five or fifteen but also at twenty-five or fifty.

---

[1]For ease and clarity, I use "mother" to refer to this close parenting relationship. However, "father" or any other loving caregiver could be appropriately substituted.

What happens during these early years also helps to shape our personal definition of trust, the cornerstone of every relationship we have and the basis for how we feel about ourselves. As I noted in my book *How Could You Do This to Me? Learning to Trust After Betrayal* (Doubleday, 1997), trust is the unspoken assumption about how we will behave toward, and be treated by, others. Without a strong foundation of trust, you're ripe for gridlock. The world remains dangerous because you don't believe inherently that someone will protect you and be there for you. Nor do you possess the confidence that you can survive on your own.

How is this foundation built? If a mother is attentive to a baby's physical and emotional needs to be loved, protected, fed, cleaned, and soothed, the child will feel comforted and safe. In time he'll come to expect that his distress signal—his crying—will bring relief. Children who know they can anticipate consistent loving care will grow up feeling happier, less anxious, and richer in self-confidence than their less fortunate counterparts, able to safely leave their parents' side to explore the world, take risks, and challenge themselves intellectually, socially, and emotionally. If they fail or encounter problems, they'll have a reservoir of self-trust and resiliency that helps them to rebound from adversity.

However, if a mother fails to respond to a baby's emotional and physical needs—if she is what I call a "not there" parent—he'll cry louder and fret longer. He'll start to feel anxious, too, because he's not entirely sure when or if, relief will come. When the foundation for trust is missing or weak, youngsters grow up worried, filled with self-doubt, and unsure of their world and their own abilities to deal with it. They may be unwilling to reach out to others, because they don't believe that anyone will be there for them.

Trust is so powerful that it will continue to play a part in every subsequent relationship you have. In love, work, or life relationships in general, you may find yourself plunged once again into an emotionally dependent position, akin to what you felt as a child. You may sense that you're following an old script, but you don't have a clue how to rewrite it so that this time, you're calling the shots. That's gridlock.

EARLY MILESTONES

According to Mahler, an infant's "psychological birth" begins around three months of age and continues until about age three. During this period every child completes a process of separating, physically as well as psychologically, from her mother as she becomes a distinct individual in her own right. In each phase of this process, the child must accomplish what mental-health experts call "developmental tasks," or milestones, that are critical for healthy emotional growth. In doing so, the child slowly gains a sense of who she is and how she can function without having to depend on others to help her.

For the purpose of this book I'm going to focus on three key stages Mahler outlined—*differentiation, practicing,* and *rapprochement*—which are where many of the gridlock problems begin. During the *differentiation* period a baby begins to notice the difference between her mother and others, comparing the familiar (that is, the mother's face) with the unfamiliar (ones she doesn't recognize). If her earlier experiences left her trustful, the baby will greet strangers with curiosity and wonderment, as well as a degree of apprehension. Without a sense of trust, she may experience stranger anxiety, becoming wary of others and again reacting with distress if anyone other than her mother picks her up or even comes too close. The infant will also repeatedly check on the mother's comings and goings and get upset if she leaves her. One place you may see the imprint of this period is in your attitude toward a spouse whose likes and dislikes are not the same as your own. Let's say your husband is very sociable and enjoys mingling at a large party but you prefer staying home with one of two couples you know well. Do you get angry and upset? Do you feel that your connection to him is somehow threatened if you don't act and feel exactly the same? If, at the party, he tells a joke that isn't very funny, do you feel embarrassed or insecure? Or are you able to laugh at his foibles without fearing that they reflect on you? Developing the ability to tolerate differences is an outgrowth of this differentiation phase, as is learning to risk expressing one's preferences without becoming overwhelmed or anxious because of them.

STEPPING OUT:
THE PRACTICING PERIOD

In the next important phase, *practicing,* the child starts to explore the world around him, first by crawling then by walking. As he begins to take steps and move away from his mother, he's filled with delight. The mother's responses during this phase are very important: If she can encourage her child to continue his exploration, his excitement overshadows any fear or anxiety he may have, as well as any frustrations he may encounter. He'll be able to hold on to his confident feelings as each new challenge or task surfaces. What's more, he'll be equipped with important life skills—among them, the confidence to act independently and take risks that call for managing anxiety in new and different situations. If you've ever been initially too shy and nervous to go to a party but mustered the courage to go anyway—telling yourself, "You know, this party will be really fun!"—you've worked through some of the issues that stem from this period.

However, if the mother is either overprotective, and holds a child back out of her own fear or worries, or is not protective enough, he may grow up fearful of new experiences and challenges. If she fails to pay sufficient attention to him, he may unwittingly get himself into trouble, since he hasn't learned to gauge appropriately the wisdom or safety of his choices and actions. It is in this period that a toddler experiences being alone, first in Mom's presence and then when she's gone. To facilitate feeling safe in her absence, he often turns to a favorite stuffed animal or blanket that has the feel or smell of Mom and uses it to calm his anxiety so he can continue to be alone and explore, even though his mother is not right beside him. This lays the foundation for adults' ability to tolerate being alone and thereby the ability to move on in a relationship.

Elliott's story shows how these basic concepts play out. A highly successful investment banker, thirty-four-year-old Elliott came to see me after breaking off his engagement to Peggy for the third time. "I know I sound like a cad," Elliott began. "I know I'm afraid of marriage. But I'm even more afraid to be alone. I don't know what will happen.

"I haven't been alone in the twelve years since college," Elliott continued. "Whenever I ended a relationship, I always made sure I had someone else waiting in the wings. Now I don't know whether I'm staying with Peggy because I can't stand to be on my own, because I feel guilty—we've been together for five years, and she tells me all the time that I'm wasting the best years of her life—or because I truly love her. How will I ever really know?"

As we spoke, Elliott began to tell me about his parents. His father was a quiet man who was steamrolled by his wife and basically let her run the show. His mother, he replied, had been dominating, possessive, and intrusive. Elliott was the last of his friends to walk to school by himself or learn to ride a bicycle, since his mother always worried that he'd get lost or hurt. He was never allowed to play on the school football team, since she deemed it too dangerous. And if he ever wanted to hang out with friends, she would inevitably find a reason he couldn't. "She'd even get angry if I was lying on my bed listening to music," Elliott reported. "She'd insist I get up and help her around her house— just like Peggy does now."

Though he didn't understand it and was uncomfortable admitting it, Elliott had never developed sufficient self-confidence to do things on his own. He related to each new girlfriend just as he had to his mother—by agreeing with and placating her for fear of being abandoned. Yet at the same time he resented their control over his life. Eventually that resentment swelled to the point that it destroyed his relationships.

YOU VERSUS THE WORLD

During the next important phase, the *rapprochement* period, the child first experiences, and learns to handle, ambivalence. The toddler who one minute insists "Yes! Me do it!" only to change her mind and insist just as emphatically that she can't, is working her way through the rapprochement phase. Because of the push-pull of independence and dependence, she may literally push Mom away, feel scared at her newfound independence, and then invest a good deal of energy trying to get Mom to return. In adults this ambivalence leads to conflicts around closeness and intimacy. The desire to be with someone while simultaneously feeling crowded—that you "need your space"—is often at the core of what looks like a lot of relationship game-playing around spending time and connecting with others. The woman who makes plans with her friends but feels guilty leaving her husband alone at night, the man who says he needs to end the relationship because he feels smothered but can't stop calling—both are feeling engulfed in much the same way as does a toddler during the rapprochement stage. This struggle rears its head, too, when you're wrestling with the decision to stay or leave a significant relationship or when you're not sure if you can function with (or without) a particular person in your life.

Another critical skill that emerges during the rapprochement period is the ability to verbalize one's needs instead of simply gesturing or wishing or assuming that one's needs will be known. Countless adults still can't say what they want when they want it. At home or at work they assume or expect that a partner, a child, a friend, a colleague, or a boss will know intuitively what they want said or done. Instead of being clear and assertive, they may manipulate and coerce others to get those needs met. Or, like Tina, whom we met in the last chapter, they may shove their own needs to the back burner. Tina baked cookies, not just to feed the school community but also to feed her own quest for love and nurturing.

Needless to say, indirect communication fuels misunderstandings and arguments. It also makes you willing to tolerate hurtful, controlling, or rejecting behavior, fearing that if you don't, you'll reexperience the early abandonment you felt with a not-there parent. And it can lead directly to the "stuck on you" behaviors I'll deal with more closely in Chapter 3, "Love Ruts."

In other words, when your early caregiver is not there for you emotionally or physically, when you don't receive the support and encouragement that ease anxiety and enable you to function and grow confidently, change of any kind may frighten, anger, or overwhelm you—and throw you into gridlock. This jumble of feelings, this emotional angst, is in fact triggered by separation anxiety—and its growing pains are by no means limited to childhood. The key is to learn to cope in a healthy, productive way with these powerful feelings. Only then can real change and growth occur.

ROLE OF A LIFETIME

The past keeps you gridlocked in yet another way: by the roles you used to play—and may continue to play—in your family. Sometimes these roles are a reflection of who you are, and sometimes they're a reflection of what others want or need you to be. For example, as the oldest child, you might have been "the big girl" or "Mommy's little helper" when it came to taking care of your younger sister. Today when that sister calls regularly with one crisis after another, you may still feel compelled to cajole her out of moods. Or perhaps this role has become so much a part of your identity that you never give a second thought to how much it is limiting and holding you back.

Labeling in and of itself is not always bad. In fact, it's necessary. We need labels to categorize information and make judgments about ourselves and our world. For parents, labeling is one way to better understand their offspring. "She's our little artist" or "He's the jock of the family" may initially be offered as a purely innocuous, even complimentary description. However, if the labels linger and a child is consistently pigeonholed into one type of behavior or role or cast in comparison to another, his image of himself may be drastically limited. Though he may choose to go along with how he's been defined, since it feels safe and secure, doing so may cut off important opportunities to pursue other talents and interests. Other times he may rage inwardly at the old labels but be unable to throw off their mantle, and in angry resignation think, "Well, if that's how they see me, that's what I'll be." The anger becomes internalized and turns self-destructive and self-defeating.

Though he didn't realize it, Kenny, a twenty-six-year-old law-school graduate, was living under a long-ago label. After graduating from law school with stellar grades, Kenny, the middle one of three boys, moved back home with his parents, but only, he told himself, for a few months until he found the right position. A year and a half later Kenny was still there, with no job prospects in sight. Though his father, himself a prominent attorney, wanted to use his connections to help his son, Kenny refused the assistance. Afraid he'd never live up to his father's expectations, and already smarting from frequent comparisons to his successful and ambitious brothers, he'd been on only five interviews. Often he'd apply for a job but fail to call for a follow-up interview.

The days soon blended together: Kenny would go to the library, ostensibly to research job opportunities; he took a course in finding a job in today's legal world and joined a support group of young law-school graduates who helped each other network. But one by one, as his peers found positions, Kenny remained gridlocked. He'd spend his days helping his parents around the house, driving his mother to her doctors' appointments and on errands, always planning that tomorrow, or next week, he'd make the phone calls he needed to make.

When he finally came to see me, Kenny was depressed and filled with self-doubt: "Maybe I just don't have what it takes to be a lawyer," he began anxiously. "How am I ever going to justify being out of work for a year and a half? I don't understand how I could let this situation get away from me like this," he admitted. "I never thought I'd stay at home this long. When I was a little kid, I was competitive, a go-getter and leader. But as I got older, I started to realize that I had a long way to go to match my older brother, Joey. If I was the star, he was the superstar, captain of the tennis and basketball teams while I was always an alternate. In so many things I'd come close to being like Joey, but a miss is as good as a mile, right? I'll never forget the gymnastic championships during my junior year. I had made it all the way to the state finals. I had one more vault to do, and as I was executing the move, I could tell that my timing was off. When I landed, my balance wavered for a split second—enough to knock me out of first place and off the roster for the rest of the season with a torn Achilles tendon. My folks used to say I reminded them of my Uncle Bill, whom I adored, by the way. Bill's a great guy, but he's the family ne'er-do-well. Everyone saw him as the black sheep. Bill had a very successful hardware and paint business, but he lost it all when the era of the megastores dawned. He wound up moving back in with my grandparents, never marrying, and taking care of them until they died. I don't want that to happen to me—but I'm afraid it has already started."

It was obvious to me that Kenny's family had much invested in his gridlock: Not only didn't they like every woman he's dated, they've been openly hostile to each one. They discouraged him from moving out. " 'There's no need. Save your money,' Dad said. 'Stay here until you find what you really like.' "

When you're stuck in an old role, you may not realize you're taking it with you into adult situations or relationships. Afraid of losing the recognition, love, or sense of identity that the role gave you, you may continue to act in ways that worked for you years ago, even though they no longer do. Just as Kenny was sent the message that he'll never really amount to anything, you, too, may not think you're smart or productive or outgoing. Typecast, your self-expression stifled, you may walk around bored and unfulfilled. As a result, you may make fewer and fewer attempts to find a job or alter an impoverished relationship, effectively sabotaging your opportunity for happiness.

PHANTOM FIGURES

And finally, the past can hold you back in the form of "phantom figures," a term I've coined to describe the significant people in your adult life with whom you unconsciously repeat the earlier experiences you had with your parents or other caregivers. Phantom figures resemble the people in your life who helped to shape your identity and self-esteem when you were young. Without realizing it, you may repeat certain experiences with these phantom people in an effort either to get the love you never had to begin with or to bring back the love you once had that was taken away.

To break out of gridlock, it's essential that you recognize the psychological impact key people have had on you—the way they affected not only how you see yourself but also how you feel about yourself. If you don't, you're likely to wind up with phantom figures, battling the same demons in your present relationships or life situations. That's because these current situations may evoke the same feelings of being controlled, undervalued, rejected, and confused that you experienced years ago. However, if you can sharpen and clarify your own sense of identity, you'll be able to respond differently to the phantom figures with whom you may be currently gridlocked—and finally get beyond the old fears, anxieties, and gnawing disappointments that have kept you trapped.

Keep in mind that phantom figures, replete with their repetition of old conflicts and emotions, can come up with different people and in a variety of settings—in friendship, at work, in love. However, each time you encounter them, you strive to recapture the love, acceptance, and approval you felt cheated out of or denied in the past. When you are in fact able to do this, phantom figures, rather than being negative, can serve as a vehicle to re-create positive loving relationships as well as to create the relationship you wished you had with a significant other and finally do attain. In this way they truly become growth-promoting.

Barbara, the multitalented woman we met at the end of Chapter 1, found a phantom figure in the form of her first cousin, Lisa, who recently moved to Boston with her husband and six-year-old daughter. Prominent figures in the music and art world, Lisa and her husband are well aware of how anxious Barbara is to get her fledgling dance company off the ground and her foot back into the cultural world. Still, while Lisa routinely calls Barbara for all kinds of help in getting her family established in a new city—and Barbara always gives it in order to win her support—Barbara's efforts have never been reciprocated. In fact, on several occasions Lisa not only denigrated Barbara's career aspirations, she sought to undercut them.

"Over the phone Lisa mentioned a job that sounded tailor-made for me, and I told her so immediately," Barbara recalled. "But she told me she didn't think I could handle it, and besides, she didn't have any clout with the director who was hiring. Months later, obviously forgetting my earlier interest, she breezily mentioned that her protégé—the woman she recommended for the spot I'd coveted—was doing fabulously. Obviously, she had hired her instead of me.

"You wouldn't believe how many times Lisa promised to set up a meeting for me with a producer or choreographer or take me to an important opening," Barbara added wistfully. "She doesn't hesitate to regale me with tales of the famous people they're having dinner with and details of the fabulous premieres they're going to. And she had the nerve to tell me that considering my age and how long I'd been out of the business, it's a pipe dream for me to even think about getting back in. Yet every time she calls at the last minute to ask if she can drop her daughter at my house for a few hours, I always say yes. When she wanted me to arrange a hard-to-get interview at my kids' private school, I did. I feel like a dope doing all this, and I wish more than anything I had the courage to tell her precisely how I feel. But I just can't. I keep thinking that maybe, just maybe, if I baby-sit her daughter four hundred times, she'll deign to arrange one measly interview for me."

Clearly Barbara is afraid to say no and forever erase the possibility that someday Lisa will come through for her. Interestingly, she didn't realize that she was acting and reacting to her cousin the same way she had toward her mother, a bitterly frustrated, insecure, and self-serving woman who routinely disparaged her daughter's abilities and achievements and saddled her with expectations so unrealistic no one could live up to them. An anecdote Barbara shared was especially telling:

"I always loved drama, and my best friend and I were constantly acting out plays or making up skits. When we were about eight or nine years old, we made a tape of us singing songs from *South Pacific* and sent it to a local television show that showcased young talent," Barbara told me, remembering how thrilled she and her friend were when they received a letter from the producer inviting them to perform on the show. "Mother was in the kitchen when I raced in with the news," Barbara continued. "She read the letter, then looked at me and said, 'Why on earth would you do such a thing? What makes you think that you have any talent?'"

It's not hard to see why Barbara today feels shadowed by self-doubt. Thirty years later she's still held back by her mother's hurtful, undermining messages. And she's still trying to win her mother's approval—literally and figuratively—in the phantom figure of her cousin Lisa. Then and now this woman who's assertive in so many areas of her life is afraid to risk alienating the one person who can bestow upon her the validation she can't give herself. Unable to let go for fear she'll then be lost, Barbara continues to strive for that ever-elusive acknowledgment through her phantom figure, Lisa.

FOREVER STUCK?

Does this mean that if you had not-there parents, who weren't sensitive and responsive, you are destined to lead a miserable, lonely life, repeating past problems over and over again? Will you never be able to undo what happened years ago or regain what might have been lost? And if you are unhappy, is it all Mom's fault?

Absolutely not. First of all, the work of Bowlby, Ainsworth, and Mahler must be understood as one of many important factors that affect healthy psychological development throughout life. Your innate abilities and talents, your experiences with your extended family—siblings and grandparents, aunts and uncles—all shape your personality and identity. So does your parents' marital relationship, as well as your connection to your peers and your teachers. Then, too, when you have a positive phantom figure, such as a boss who gives you the love and support your father never did, that mentoring relationship can boost your confidence and your career.

What's more, by shining a light on the early years, you'll be able to see more clearly which areas you need to strengthen to better handle potentially destructive feelings. That's the first step toward unlearning the attitudes and behaviors that keep you gridlocked and honing new ones that allow you to move forward successfully and independently.

WHAT'S YOUR GQ?
TAKE THE GRIDLOCK QUESTIONNAIRE

The short quiz that follows provides a statistically reliable and valid measurement of the degree to which you have successfully completed the separation/individuation process that is fundamental to healthy emotional growth. With the results in hand, you'll be able to pinpoint how secure and independent you are. You'll also be able to recognize your propensity for gridlock as well as understand which emotions are making you feel so trapped. The results of the Gridlock Questionnaire are pivotal: A high score suggests that the hidden roadblocks from your past may still be robbing you of initiative and keeping you locked in old, unworkable patterns that, despite your best efforts, you're unable to break. A low score means you have successfully worked through some of these issues.

Below you'll find a set of statements that adults often make. Most people agree with some of them, but very few people agree with all of them. Read each of the statements and indicate in the blank to the left of the statement if you agree or disagree that it describes you (+ means you agree; − means you disagree) and how strongly you feel about it (1 equals slightly; 2 equals moderately; 3 equals strongly).

Note: Ratings go after each numbered statement.

+ 1 agree slightly
+ 2 agree moderately
+ 3 agree strongly
− 1 disagree slightly
− 2 disagree moderately
− 3 disagree strongly

1. People I am close to should know what makes me happy without my telling them. _____
2. I'm very anxious when I am with people I don't know very well.
3. I often go out of my way to meet potentially interesting people whom I don't already know. _____
4. I tend to be stubborn about getting things I want. _____
5. When I was in school, I did my best to win my teacher's favor. _____
6. I don't mind compromising in order to share my friends' or spouse's interests and hobbies. _____
7. I feel guilty whenever I leave someone. _____
8. When I get upset, I really need to have someone reassure me that things will be all right again. _____
9. For me, a very important part of being loved is to be caressed and embraced. _____
10. I easily get angry when things don't go my way. _____
11. I always feel responsible for the way other people are feeling. _____
12. I don't feel understood if I must tell someone what it is that pleases me. _____
13. I tend to quarrel with others when their preferences are different from mine. _____
14. When I am anxious, I tend to eat or drink or smoke to settle myself down. _____
15. I can't stand when someone criticizes me. _____
16. I feel (felt) responsible for my mother's happiness. _____
17. It's hard for me to accept my mistakes and try again. _____
18. I usually have a very difficult time when I am faced with having to make a decision. _____
19. I often feel misunderstood. _____

20. I get anxious whenever the person closest to me goes away, even for a short time. _____
21. I am not really comfortable meeting strangers, even when I am accompanied by the person with whom I feel the closest. _____
22. When I was younger, I was extremely attached to one favorite item—a blanket or toy—and hated being separated from it. _____
23. I am easily disappointed. _____
24. It is difficult for me to know what someone's needs are unless they verbalize them to me. _____
25. It is difficult for me to independently start new activities that might interest me. _____
26. I get quite anxious whenever I am in conflict with someone with whom I am close. _____
27. I am very self-critical. _____
28. I feel (felt) responsible for my father's happiness. _____
29. I often feel guilty when I do what I want to do. _____
TOTAL _____

If you have a high score (between 98 and 168), you are most likely grid-locked by one or more of the following feelings—anxiety, fear, guilt, ambivalence, and anger—which makes it difficult for you to move independently in some area of your life.

For example, you could be gridlocked by *anxiety*. When you're anxious, your heightened sense of danger signals you to stop. Without knowing how to reassure yourself that some degree of unease is a normal emotional growing pain, you come to a grinding halt.

Then, too, a host of *fears* may be your biggest roadblock to change. If you're afraid to be alone, it may be gridlocking you in a relationship you know you've outgrown. If you're afraid of independence, you may be reluctant to try new things or push yourself professionally, even though you feel stifled and unchallenged in your work. The longer you remain stuck, the more convinced you are that your fears are unconquerable.

Or you may be swamped by *guilt*. You may be uncomfortable expressing your needs and worry that doing so is selfish. Instead, you feel much more responsible for other people's well-being than for your own. You take care of them before taking care of yourself, at great expense to your self-esteem.

You may also discover that you can't decide whether to leave a relationship or quit a job. Every time you feel strongly one way, your feelings shift, and you're unable to resolve the conflicting thoughts swirling in your head. Stuck in neutral, you're gridlocked by *ambivalence*.

And finally, if you have difficulty expressing *anger*, you may hold it in and then become depressed. Or your emotional road rage may erupt in temper tantrums, never knowing when you're going to lose control or whom you're going to hit.

A low GQ score, on the other hand (between 28 and 98), indicates that you are well equipped to function independently:

- You greet new experiences and people with curiosity, confidence, and enthusiasm.
- You're able to handle being alone and acting independently, still feeling safe and protected.
- You're able to begin something new—a job, a relationship, a different way of acting within an ongoing relationship—and at the same time manage the confusing, frightening feelings that inevitably surface as you take a step toward change.
- You're able to manage ambivalent feelings by making decisive choices that lead to action, instead of waffling and remaining stuck.
- You're able to use your anger constructively, to ask for what you want and need without guilt holding you back. You won't tolerate hurtful, controlling, or rejecting behavior out of fear that if you don't, you'll be abandoned and reexperience the feelings of loss you felt years ago.

So where are you gridlocked? In the following chapters I'll delineate the specific ruts most likely to keep you stuck. Once you know where and why you're trapped, I'll give you specific directions for confronting your fears, taming your anxiety and guilt, harnessing your anger and intuition—and jump-starting your life.

CHAPTER THREE

LOVE RUTS

"I've had it," said Claire, thirty-six, the mother of two preteen sons, as she described her eleven-year marriage to Doug, a business executive. "I'm tired of feeling unimportant, tired of doing everything for and with the kids, tired of asking Doug to share part of the responsibility, even part of his life, with me. I do believe he *thinks* he is—that's the problem. It's simply not enough."

Married at twenty-three, Claire quit law school at the end of her freshman year to stay home with her two sons, born fourteen months apart. While Doug completed his M.B.A., Claire slipped comfortably into full-time motherhood. "Initially I really didn't mind doing everything," she recalled. "I was just so excited to be married and raising these two wonderful kids. I grew up in a large, close family—we all still live within a few blocks of each other, and I love it that way. My parents, sisters, and assorted cousins are always running in and out of each other's homes. But after a few years I think the newness of it all wore thin. Instead of being a joy, taking care of the children became a burden. I'm always on duty, evenings and weekends. Doug comes home late from the office, picks up the remote, starts channel-surfing, and falls asleep in the chair. On weekends he never sees any reason he can't play golf or basketball with his friends instead of giving me a few hours off or being with me for a change. 'Your mother or your sisters can watch them, can't they? Why are you hassling me?' he'll say. Of course my parents are delighted to see their grandchildren; that's not the point. Marriage should be a partnership."

Doug doesn't know how to share his world either. "I'll ask about his day, but he brushes me off and says he doesn't like to talk about the office," she explained. "And he certainly doesn't want to hear about my day. As soon as I say, 'We have to talk,' he acts as if I've thrown a hand grenade at him, and he runs for cover. After a while I gave up trying to get him to understand. But I've never stopped being angry.

"Doug prides himself on being laid-back and accommodating, but he really does only what he wants to do when he wants to do it," Claire continued. "I can't tell you all the things he's promised to do but never got around to. Eventually I got so resentful that just hearing his key turn in the lock made me tense and irritated." Even Doug's lovemaking had a selfish quality to it. "Every Saturday night we have sex; you could set your watch by it," Claire added. "But he doesn't think about being romantic or tender, and I don't think he gives a second thought to whether I feel good. He has his orgasm, goes through the motions of pleasuring me, and falls asleep. I lie there staring at the ceiling and wondering how on earth I'm going to get through the next thirty years. No one in my family has ever divorced or even separated. What am I going to do?"

Claire is gridlocked in a love rut. She's married to someone who's not loving her back the way she wants to be loved. She's tried to resolve the problems with Doug, but they remain polarized. She's tried to accept things for what they are, to focus her energy on other matters, but it's getting harder and harder to remember why she fell in love in the first place. And she can't decide whether to stay or leave.

Love ruts are as varied as the people and relationships in which they are gridlocked. You can be stuck in a love rut when you're just beginning a new relationship, when you're well into a relationship, even long after you thought you'd finally ended a relationship. Elliott, whom you met in the last chapter, gets cold feet as soon as his wedding date approaches and inevitably finds a reason to postpone the ceremony. Rebecca, whom you'll soon meet, always falls for men who are unavailable: Either they live in a distant city or are married to their work—or to someone else. And Christine is so enraged by her former husband's infidelity and refusal even to try to save their twenty-three-year marriage that two years after her divorce she still finds it difficult to let another man into her life. They're all gridlocked in a love rut.

Love ruts evolve slowly, over time. Whenever you sense that a partner isn't fully there for you—if he or she doesn't listen when you want to talk, makes promises but rarely keeps them, appears uninterested in activities or pursuits you enjoy, or deprecates the things, large or small, that are vital to you—you may become confused, angry, or even guilt-ridden. You know you don't feel like yourself, or good about yourself, when you're with this person, yet you can't make sense of the conflicting messages you keep getting. You ignore minor misgivings, overlook even legitimate signs of trouble. Most damaging of all, you question your perceptions and doubt the validity of your needs.

To help you cope with this swirl of uncomfortable feelings, you unconsciously slip into a love rut: You may cling too tightly to a partner who is not right for you, minimize or deny that there's anything wrong, or distance yourself from your mate emotionally or physically. You may even become passionately involved with a new lover, yet be unable to give up the old.

Love ruts keep you in a holding pattern. Hooked on the illusion of love and security or on the misguided belief that since no relationship is ever perfect, your expectations are undoubtedly too high, you downplay the negatives. You want so much to be open, enthusiastic, hopeful. Still, you vacillate and wonder: Are the problems really so bad, the hurts so unpardonable? Isn't there anything you could do, some way this relationship could be saved?

Love ruts obscure the clarity you need to decide what's best. Like Claire, you may miss the warning signs that a relationship is dead-ended and linger for years in an unsatisfying marriage that slowly chips away at your dreams and your self-esteem. On the other hand, you may see the danger signs quite clearly—a partner's addiction to drugs or alcohol or even his outright insistence that he's not interested in a committed relationship—but instead of making concrete changes that will resolve your confusion and end your pain, you assume you can change him. Or you take that knowledge, file it away, and forget about it. Consciously or unconsciously, you sabotage your chances at love and keep yourself stuck.

HOOKED ON THE PAST . . .

As we saw in Chapter 2, the past can keep you gridlocked in a love rut in ways that are so subtle you may find it hard to believe they still have an impact. Unmet emotional needs from childhood do live on, as you strive to find a partner who will provide you with the understanding and intimacy you've longed for but never found. Phantom figures—people who remind you of those who were instrumental in your psychological and emotional development—turn up in the faces of lovers or spouses, confounding you with the mixed feelings you have for them when you're with them. Indeed, the arguments you're having with your partner today may actually be the same old ones—for approval, for control, to be listened to—that you waged with your parents years ago and still can't get beyond.

Early but critical losses—a separation, a divorce, or a parent who was domineering or distant—set the stage for future difficulties in love relationships, where trust is a critical factor. You may be anxious about getting too close to someone and peeling bare your deepest feelings, or so sensitive to rejection that you cling too tightly to whoever shows you the slightest attention. Or you may be so emotionally needy that you crave affection and move from one mediocre relationship to another, distrusting your judgment and rendering yourself vulnerable to hurt, even betrayal.

Many people gridlocked in love are particularly puzzled by their ability to function well in one area of life—at work, with their children, or in myriad community or vocational activities—while their romantic lives remain in shambles. Once again, those leftover issues and conflicts may be so powerful that they throw you off balance and prevent you from forging a healthy, solid relationship built on respect and sealed with empathy. Instead, you accept disappointment, mistreatment, and rejection as your lot in life. Or you try so frantically to maintain a relationship that isn't working, you forget that you actually have a better option: You can leave.

. . . OR IN THE PRESENT

Money and sex can also chain people to unrewarding, dead-ended relationships. When studies report that a woman's income drops precipitously after divorce, it's hard to discount the economic realities that force many wives to struggle at keeping bad marriages afloat. "When we first had kids, we both agreed that I'd quit my job to be home full-time," explains Andrea, thirty-eight, the mother of a thirteen-year-old daughter and a ten-year-old son, whose husband, Warren, has been repeatedly unfaithful during their fifteen years together. "We didn't want anyone else to raise our children. But now Warren has a very successful dental practice, and I haven't been in the workforce for fifteen years. What am I supposed to write on my résumé—Mommy? There's no way I can ever survive on my own." As you'll soon understand, women like Andrea are gridlocked in the Staller rut.

What's more, providing financial support to a partner gives the provider a big self-esteem boost as well as a security deposit on his or her emotional well-being. "It does make me feel needed," admitted Myra, forty-five, a cosmetics executive who every year pours thousands of dollars into her mate's small newsletter company. "I suppose on some level I've always known that Peter would never pay me back," she added, "but initially I didn't see why it mattered who paid for what. Besides, it's hard to say no when someone tells you they'd do the same for you if the situation was reversed." But over time Myra has begun to resent the direction their relationship has taken. "When we first started seeing each other, I'd pay for the occasional dinner or theater ticket. No big deal. Now I'm paying for all that, plus his clothes and our vacations, too," she says. Myra can't deny that she is more secure knowing that she's bankrolling Peter's life; after all, as long as he's financially dependent on her, she knows he's not going to leave. On the other hand, she hates the fact that she's buying his love.

Like money, sexual passion can be the glue that keeps you grid-locked in a love rut. Many people mistake lust and attraction for real love and intimacy. "I know he ignores me when we're with other people, and I see him eyeing every woman who walks in the room," said Michelle, twenty-four, describing the current man in her life. "But our lovemaking is terrific. It's hard to imagine that the relationship isn't. In bed he makes me feel like I'm the only one he cares about." What's more, great sex has a way of triggering selective amnesia. "I've stayed married to Matthew all these years primarily because we're good in bed," thirty-eight-year-old Jenna told me frankly. "We have a solid sex life, and that helps me forget and ignore a lot. Call me hypocritical, but I don't want to give that up. The bedroom is one place where I feel confident and good about myself."

Are you gridlocked in love? How can you tell if you're really trapped—or if you and a partner have just hit a rocky stretch of road? People are torn apart by ambivalence, the simultaneous attraction toward and turning away from a person that leads to fluctuating feelings of love and hate. The way they manage these powerful, ambivalent feelings often leads to "stuck on you" behaviors—clinging, stalling, distancing, and bouncing—that determine the type of love rut in which they become gridlocked. Let's take a closer look at the most common love ruts, the Stoplights that hold you there, as well as the various dead-end lovers who are most damaging to your sense of self.

LOVE RUT # 1: CLINGERS

"I CAN'T LIVE WITH HIM—OR WITHOUT HIM."

"Within hours of meeting Tim, I knew he was selfish and full of himself. I'd met men like him before; I knew the type well," recalled Rebecca, a thirty-nine-year-old attorney. "But for some reason I ignored every warning signal. Tim was witty, smart, and sexy—as my secretary said, 'a good catch.' I wanted it to work so much. I guess I believed for a long time that he was the right one for me."

Rebecca first met Tim, an advertising salesman, at a fund-raising dinner. "Though I told him I had to leave early to prepare for a case the next day, he came on strong and kept insisting that I join him for a late drink," she related. She went, and three months later he had unofficially moved into her apartment.

But it never felt right. If they went to a party or dinner, Tim always spent far more time flirting with other women or trying to get her clients to invest in his new business projects than he did with her. When colleagues offered Rebecca tickets to the theater or ballet, Tim rarely had a free evening. But if those tickets were for a hockey or basketball game, he managed to squeeze in the time. Even his gifts seemed more for his pleasure than for hers: For Christmas *and* her birthday, Tim, a fitness fanatic, bought her Nike running shoes—the latest model, but not exactly what she'd hoped for. "I've jogged maybe three times in my life," she said, sighing. "He didn't even notice that my enthusiasm hardly matched his."

Although her friends hinted that Tim was taking advantage of her, Rebecca made excuses for him. "It's funny. At work I consider myself a great judge of character. I can psych out witnesses and judges, finesse an argument to win my point. But with Tim I'm completely flustered. If I try to tell him how I feel, he turns things inside out, so I wind up feeling like I'm not doing enough—or apologizing to him for being bitchy and expecting too much. 'You're the one I'm with, not those other women. Why are you so jealous?' he'll say. Or 'You're just being paranoid.' He actually thinks everything is fine with us! But I always sacrifice so he can feel comfortable. Because he moved in with me, I do the shopping, the cooking, the cleaning, plus pay the rent. I used to tell myself I'd be doing all that anyway, but lately I can't help wondering what I'm getting out of it. Nothing feels balanced."

It wasn't until Rebecca needed surgery to fix torn cartilage in her knee and Tim was unable to juggle his schedule to pick her up at the hospital that she finally conceded she'd once again picked a man who placed her far down on his priority list. Nevertheless, when she came to see me, Rebecca was convinced that there was something wrong with her. "Why can't I make this relationship work? Why do I always find guys like this? I keep thinking that one day he'll really listen and hear me, one day he'll be as emotionally tuned in to me as I try to be for him. It's hard to come to terms with the fact that he doesn't seem to give a damn about me." In the back of her mind is the despairing thought that self-centered Tim might be as good as it's ever going to get—and if he finds someone else, it's proof that the woman he chooses is better than Rebecca. Rebecca is a typical Clinger. Clingers are gridlocked in a fire-and-ice relationship, and their intensely ambivalent feelings toward a partner dominate their lives. When a mate is unavailable or hurtful, they become so angry that the relationship feels untenable, and they convince themselves that they are fools for remaining in it. However, as soon as a partner behaves in a loving way—and at times, they do—the Clinger swings to the other end of the pendulum and believes she can't possibly live without this person in her life.

Some Clingers desperately want to be married, but they feel time is running out. That's why they'll hang on to Mr. Wrong or Mr. Not-Quite-Right and rarely admit, even to themselves, that a relationship they've spent years trying to fix was never good from the start. Overwhelmed by their need to find someone to love them back, Clingers like Rebecca say yes too often and too easily. They lack the ability to discriminate and will often sacrifice emotional fulfillment to keep a man, any man, by their side. Should anyone cast doubt on the relationship, the Clinger has a ready explanation: "Well, he can be so wonderful sometimes. . . . As soon as we work through this one issue, I know things will be better." Deep down, however, the Clinger fears she's unworthy and unlovable and will never find what she's searching for. So she swallows her expectations along with her pride and rationalizes that it's smarter to settle for what she has than to hunt in vain.

Ironically, a Clinger who is single is often attracted to commitment-phobic lovers and will consistently miss the cues that signal that this person is, and probably always will be, emotionally unavailable. Not only does the Clinger convince herself that through her continuous love and support she will be the one woman to turn this guy around; she feels guilty if she doesn't do everything in her power to try. Unable to distinguish between actions that are self-preserving and those that are selfish, blind to a lover's limitations, the Clinger can't see that what she does or doesn't do is really of little significance. This guy behaves the same way with everybody.

If you're single and have been in a lengthy relationship with someone who makes promises and speaks to the future but backs off the minute you try to pin him down, you're a Clinger. If you're doing 90 percent of the giving and he's doing 100 percent of the taking, you, too, are a Clinger. If you're divorced but still in love with your ex-spouse and unable to let go of him, you may be one as well. In fact, the Clinger is so overwhelmed at the prospect of going it alone that she is easily fooled by a former spouse's sporadic efforts to reconnect in some way.

But here's the paradox for people stuck in the Clinger rut: Even though your lover lets you down, or refuses to make a lasting commitment, at times he does seem to want and care for you. It may not be often, or consistently, but it's enough to allow you to block out the distress you're experiencing and, for a while, actually forget it. Christine, whom I mentioned at the beginning of this chapter, has been divorced for two years, but her ex-husband still calls her on her birthday, still drops over to make sure the boiler isn't giving her any trouble, and on his way out the door still tenderly grasps her arm as he bends to kiss her good-bye. Visits like these rekindle Christine's hope that perhaps he really does love her after all, and she clings to the belief that maybe, just maybe, they'll get back together.

What's more, not only does the Clinger cling, she has a partner who holds on tight. It's not uncommon to discover that, once she finally reaches her limit and makes an effort to break away, a Clinger's partner suddenly needs and wants her more than ever and will fight fiercely to win her back. Repetitive phone calls, apologies, and promises to change seduce the Clinger right back into her love rut.

STOPLIGHT: SEPARATION ANXIETY AND FEAR OF THE UNKNOWN

Clingers have so many leftover childhood needs that they hold on to a relationship at all costs—denying, minimizing, and ultimately not even seeing what is clear to everyone else. What enables Clingers to tolerate such profound emptiness? Because they never learned to differentiate their needs from those of their partner, they experience a partner's needs as their own. Though at times they may have an inkling of their own true preferences, if and when they voice them, it usually leads to conflict. So they learn to suppress them and instead take on the role of caretaker in a relationship. By doing this, they actually feel as if they are taking care of themselves. In essence, the Clinger grows up believing she is loved for what she does, not for who she is. Interestingly, Clingers are frequently attracted to partners who just as desperately need someone to take care of them. The person addicted to drugs or alcohol, for example, depends on someone to cater to his needs—precisely what the Clinger wants and needs to do to whitewash her own emptiness.

For a Clinger, being with a person who can't or won't give you the love you need probably feels familiar. Perhaps your father was unavailable—traveling on business, divorced from your mother, or overly demanding and critical. Or perhaps your mother made you well aware of the fact that she'd sacrificed her career goals to raise children. In either case you received the message that you and your needs weren't important, and that it was wise to put them aside in favor of someone else's. To win your parents' love and acceptance, you may have focused on being good and keeping the family peace. You're probably doing the same thing now in every love relationship: By bending over backward to please a partner, even supporting him financially, you're trying to earn the approval you need to feel better about yourself.

In fact, a Clinger is so fearful of being independent and so anxious for validation, she'll often merge her identity with a partner's. What he likes, she likes; what he wants to do, she wants to do. The Clinger confuses what she can realistically expect from a partner. With self-esteem based so profoundly on another's acceptance, voicing one's own wishes or preferences invokes tremendous anxiety. The risk of disapproval—and ultimately rejection—is simply too great. Inevitably Clingers wind up doing most of the giving—or the giving in.

A Clinger also gets stuck because she's still trying to prove her independence from a parent who heightens her insecurities by criticizing her choices or questioning her still-single lifestyle. "You're not getting any younger, you know," Mother might say. "And you've always been too picky. What are you waiting for?" Though you may recognize that a partner is inconsiderate, even dishonest, you can't forget Mother's prophecy, and it's easy to lose sight of what's important to you.

That's what's gridlocking Patsy, a graphic artist in her mid-thirties, who came to me distressed and puzzled by her poor romantic track record. Patsy's modus operandi never varied: She'd date a man for several months, but as soon as they began to talk about moving in together, she'd begin to find fault with him. An only child whose father died when she was sixteen, Patsy had always discussed her love life with her mother, who, despite her insistence that marriage be every woman's goal, criticized in scathing detail each man her daughter dated. He wasn't making enough money, he lived too far away, he had an ex-wife who was too demanding, or his hair was funny. Inevitably Patsy would argue with her mother and defend her choices, but she always wound up seeing her lover through her mother's eyes. While she knew she should not accept her mother's values, she couldn't figure out what her own were. Even at her age she was still seeking Mom's approval—and sabotaging her own chances at love. Consequently her lovers became the pawn through which Patsy continued to battle her mother and assert her independence.

Being stuck in old childhood roles can also render someone more susceptible to being gridlocked in the Clinger rut. Annette, the oldest of five children, raised her siblings when her mother was killed in an airplane crash. Then eighteen, Annette dealt with the loss of her mother by mothering her younger brothers and sisters. Not only did she believe she had to do this for their well-being, she wanted to. Filling her mother's shoes was one way to keep her memory close, and Annette's sense of self-worth became inextricably bound to how well she took care of her siblings. Now thirty-three, she continues to minister to their needs—hammering out their marriage problems, loaning them money, or giving up her nights and weekends to baby-sit. She has yet to find a man who doesn't feel squeezed out by her devotion to her family. Ironically, Annette wants to get married and is depressed about how unlucky in love she is. What she doesn't see is that she's left no room in her heart, or her life, for anyone but her siblings.

Rebecca's old childhood role as the do-gooder and caretaker of her older brother, Ben, carried over into her phantom-figure relationship with her boyfriend, Tim. Growing up, she had to fend off Ben's outrageous demands and unwarranted criticism. If she tried to defend herself, he'd make her feel that she was being selfish, immature, or unloving. Even now, when her brother bombards her with requests for favors from her business contacts, Rebecca finds it hard to say no. Her herculean efforts to please her lover Tim mirror the relationship she still has with Ben. "They say 'Jump,' and I always say 'How high?'" she admitted.

- You're so hooked on the hope that the relationship will become fulfilling, it blinds you to how empty it is.
- No matter how successful and happy you are in other parts of your life, unless you're with this man, you don't feel complete.
- You don't trust your own judgment and often allow the opinions of a parent or lover to overshadow your own.
- When you do act independently or voice your ideas and preferences, you become extremely anxious.

LOVE RUT #2: STALLERS

"IT'S NOT SO BAD."

Although Jackie had been unhappy for over a decade, she didn't realize how deep her despair was. Like Rebecca, she believed she was being selfish, demanding, and unappreciative. "I have so much," began Jackie, who's been married to Jeff, her high-school sweetheart, for eighteen years. "Two terrific kids, a beautiful home, the financial resources to live the way we want, a husband who says he adores me. But I feel empty. I know my marriage is what a good marriage should be."

A stunning blonde who looks much like the cheerleader she once was, Jackie wed Jeff the week after they graduated from college. "I know it's not politically correct to say this, but all I really wanted was to be a wife and mom," she conceded. As Jeff, a computer wizard, poured his time and energy into his fledgling software company, Jackie "out–Martha Stewart–ed Martha Stewart," as she put it. "I'd string thousands of cranberries to make holiday wreaths, bake bread from scratch, drive my kids and their friends everywhere. Almost every night I'd prepare a lovely meal for my husband." Jeff would sing her praises to anyone who'd listen, Jackie told me. "He put me on a pedestal and let the whole world know it. I thought he was a terrific husband and father, and so did everyone else. And what people think is very important to me," she said.

But on weekends or holidays Jeff was never far from his cell phone or fax, and Jackie frequently felt like a single parent, going alone to school conferences or functions. "I used to tell myself that he had a lot on his plate. Could I really expect him to drop everything to come to the second-grade production of *Peter Pan*?" Over time, though, he missed so many special occasions, she could no longer find an excuse. Nor could she overlook the fact that everything in their lives revolved around Jeff. "Since he was working so hard, I thought that letting him decide what we should do on the weekend was the least I could do. If one of the kids wanted to attend a friend's birthday party but Jeff had deemed that day perfect for a movie . . . well, the party was history. I had to push him to visit his parents, or even call his mother. In a way, I made it easy for him. If things didn't go well, he had someone to blame—me."

Jackie also started to feel resentful and smothered by her husband's possessiveness. "He wanted to be with me, and me alone"—but that didn't include tuning in to *her* needs. "When I had the flu and was literally flat on my back for a week, I naturally expected Jeff to take over but he didn't," Jackie recalled. "He said he had to work, so I had to recruit friends to carpool the kids and make dinner. Another time I had two kids home with the chicken pox at once, and he couldn't understand why I was frazzled. That's when I knew I was stuck. But what could I do? There was only one road for me. I had no work skills. Where was I going to go?"

Recently, when Jeff's business hit a rocky period, Jackie bore the brunt of his anger. "He called me lazy and disorganized and had the audacity to imply that because I wasn't rushing out to find a job, I must not have much self-esteem," she reported. Still, no matter how wounded Jackie was, she rarely raised her voice in anger. "That's not who I am, or how I was brought up," she says. "Not that it would have made a difference. If I tried to confront him, he walked away, telling me to keep my voice down so I didn't upset the kids. 'We'll talk about it later,' he'd say." But later never came.

Jackie continued to play the part of the good wife—making dinner, doing the laundry—but she began refusing to have sex. "Jeff couldn't see that I didn't want to make love because of the way he was treating me," she said. "He blamed me and my 'hormone problems.'" For the first time Jackie started to fantasize about what life might be like if she were married to someone else, but quickly brushed those thoughts aside.

"Maybe my marriage isn't what I'd like it to be, but how many people are ecstatically happy after all these years?" she reminded herself.

Jackie is a Staller—and Stallers are nothing if not stoical. They deal with their ambivalence toward a partner by denying it, and instead of focusing on any bad, they block it out and focus only on the good. Like Clingers, Stallers come slowly to the realization that they're in a warped relationship. They expend so much energy stifling their resentment and maintaining the myth of their perfect marriage that they can actually keep their frustration at bay for indefinite periods of time. Stallers miss the obvious and forgive too easily, because over time they've become emotionally numb. What's the point of staying angry? they tell themselves. However, by ignoring their anger, they often wind up internalizing it and becoming depressed. Periodically they make halfhearted attempts to express their feelings—by fretting, complaining, or even going so far as threatening to leave a partner unless changes are made. But the threats are idle, the ultimatums hollow. In truth, a Staller knows she's not going anywhere—and so does her partner—because she has too much to lose.

A Staller puts everyone's needs ahead of her own; in this way she feels indispensable and applauded. Pouring every ounce of energy into her children's well-being, she's often exhausted at the end of the day and wants nothing more than a few hours of time alone. In a way, the fact that her husband is not around becomes a relief. Since the Staller usually believes that her unfulfilling relationship is primarily her fault, she feels guilty wishing for or expecting more. Still, she can't stop trying. Maybe she felt that she wasn't the good enough daughter, but she'll make damn sure she's the good enough spouse.

If you're gridlocked in the Staller rut, the past is the only reason you're staying in the present. You rationalize unhappiness by reminding yourself that you've already invested so much in this relationship, you can't possibly let it go. Practical matters probably complicate the picture, and you focus on them: the children, your history together, the business the two of you started from scratch, your desire to maintain the lifestyle you enjoy. If you do implement change, you're always lured back by a spouse who triggers your deepest insecurities and guilt. After all, if you keep hearing "Most women would trade places with you in a second" or "What do you have to be so unhappy about? Look at all I give you," it's hard not to doubt yourself. Besides, when life is going smoothly, you may feel safe and even loved. You don't realize you're holding a parachute that will never open.

STOPLIGHT: THE FEAR OF BEING ALONE AND UNLOVABLE

Stallers often use their partner as a vehicle to help them separate from family pressures and ties. But the separation is incomplete, and they still don't fully trust their own feelings, opinions, and instincts. As a result, they turn to a spouse for the stamp of approval. The Staller needs her parents' blessing less only because she needs her partner's more.

Like the Clinger, the Staller probably had not-there parents who made her feel that no matter how accommodating or accomplished she was, it wasn't enough. Maybe you were smart—but your sister was smarter. Perhaps you sacrificed time with your friends to be with your parents—but in their eyes you could have done more. Or perhaps, like Jackie, you were the favored child, praised and rewarded for how well you adhered to Mom's advice and guidance. Jackie's older brother, the family rebel, barely graduated from high school, hung out with the wrong crowd, and was frequently in trouble. "Thank God I have a daughter like you," Jackie's mother used to tell her. "At least you don't make us crazy and hurt our feelings the way your brother does." Jackie learned that the way to gain love was to squash her true feelings. She also had a reputation to live up to. Now, Jeff—the phantom figure in her life—is treating her much the same way her parents did. But since she was taught that expressing her feelings honestly was one of the worst things she could do, Jackie resigns herself to whatever her husband wants. Being a doormat is far less anxiety-provoking than standing up for herself.

Donna, forty-five, the mother of three, faced a similar dilemma, and her response to it was different, though no less typical for a Staller. Donna had always wanted to write children's books, and she still gets angry just thinking about how her father routinely and condescendingly discouraged her from pursuing what he called "fanciful notions."

"Dad would bellow, 'You want to be a starving writer?'" Donna explained. "He insisted that I take business and even secretarial courses so I could get a job when I graduated from college. If I disagreed with him, he wouldn't talk to me for days."

When Donna married Brad, an investment banker, she tabled her dreams of writing and settled, happily, into a suburban life—for a while. But after her youngest son entered middle school, Donna had more free time, and she started to think again about writing. She enrolled in a writing seminar that met two evenings a week and every other Saturday. Brad was furious.

"Look, I'm not insensitive," he insisted. "I know my work is consuming, and that's exactly why, when I come home, I want to be with her. I'm not asking her to cook dinner every night—I'll take her out! I just want to spend time with *her*. Why is that asking too much? Doesn't she want to be with me?" As with every Staller, Donna's guilt buttons are easily accessible—and Brad knew just how to push them. She was furious at his objections, but instead of kowtowing to her husband and dropping her writing seminar—as Jackie might have done—Donna went every week, and either lied to her husband about where she was going or threw a childish tantrum. She sulked, sobbed, and shouted— just as she had with her father—until Brad caved in. Like all Stallers, Donna didn't know how to channel her anger to negotiate her own needs like a grown-up. She may think she's taking charge of her life by arguing with her husband or lying to him. But like Jackie, she's as stuck as she ever was.

YOU'RE GRIDLOCKED HERE IF . . .

- You're hooked on security and afraid to jeopardize the lifestyle you now have.
- You feel you have no control over your life. You're powerless to make decisions because you're dependent financially or emotionally on your spouse.
- Instead of focusing on what you're not getting in your marriage, you accept your partner's view of all that you have and all that he's giving you.
- You've been on the verge of ending this relationship several times, but for some reason—always a very good one—you back down and stay put.

LOVE RUT #3: DISTANCERS

"WHY AM I STILL SINGLE?"

"I've never had a problem meeting women," Dan, a thirty-seven-year-old sportswear manufacturer told me. "I've just never found the right one. Sometimes I'll date three or four women at a time, but I always find reasons they aren't right. I run down my mental checklist: Is she smart enough? Pretty enough?"

For a long time Dan reveled in his single life. "You know what they say, 'So many women, so little time.' I liked playing the field. And most of my friends were single. But last year I went to five weddings. I started to wonder if there was something wrong with me. I never thought my standards were too high, but now I'm not so sure. I don't want to sound like I'm bragging, but I know there are several women who would marry me in a minute. The problem is, I can't see spending my life with any of them."

During the past ten years Dan has haderious relationships with three women; he'd pursue each one ardently until he caught her. But sooner or later—usually sooner—he'd feel smothered and dis-contented. One woman wasn't ambitious enough. Another was too in-volved in her own career to pay much attention to him and his. Still another was cute and smart but "just too negative. She stressed out about everything," he explained.

Dan always finds a deal-breaker. "I'll fall hard for a woman, the sex will be great. But as soon as she talks about moving in, I'll start picking stupid fights over ridiculous issues," he admitted. "Women tell me I'm afraid of commitment. I don't think that's it. I just don't want to be stuck in a marriage like my parents', living with someone because I feel I should, not because I want to."

Those are high-minded words, to be sure, and they made Dan feel better about himself—for a while. By the time he found his way to my office, though, he had conceded that something was wrong. He just couldn't figure out what.

Dan is a Distancer. He thinks he wants to be in a lasting relation-ship; in fact, he relishes the pursuit. The trouble is, he's terrified of being caught. His girlfriends are right: He *is* afraid of commitment and displays all the symptoms of the proverbial guy who gets cold feet, though he denies it vociferously and is puzzled by the label. Distancers don't want to be single forever; they just want to be single for now. But "now" soon becomes "always." Dan, for instance, falls in love but never stays in love, always discovering a flaw that makes each woman, each relationship, all wrong.

Distancers' journeys toward love are one step forward, two steps back. They often choose partners who are in some way unavailable: married to someone else, married to their work, living in another city, or as afraid of commitment as they are. But ironically, because of their own reservations, they either don't see or overlook the flashing warning signs. The Distancer and the Distancee are a good fit: Each works to maintain a much-needed zone of safety. In this way they never have to take the relationship too seriously and run the risk of becoming too involved—or too hurt. Those who have already been emotionally bruised by a bad marriage often fall into the Distancer rut as well. Desperately afraid of putting themselves on the emotional firing line again, they erect protective barriers.

Some Distancers are involved with one person over a long period of time, with many on-again/off-again breakups that last for days or weeks. Others are serial seducers, abandoning their partners with little warning or with the most banal explanations. In either case they believe that unless a relationship is perfect, it's all wrong. One misstep, one fight, is a sure sign that they've made a horrendous mistake. Rather than try to work it out, they pull away.

Quick to anger, Distancers use any disagreement as reason enough to rupture the relationship. Though they may make repeated efforts to heal the break, they lack the skills and capacity to handle their anger, frustration, and disappointment, as well as the ability to empathize and communicate in an open, honest way. For them, being close feels like control, and the last thing they want to be is accountable to anyone. Sharing feels like obligation, compromise like sacrifice—one they're unwilling and unable to make.

Distancers' relationships are punctuated by differences and misunderstandings. However, because they don't understand the roots of their ambivalence, they're unable to sort through their feelings and put them in perspective. In fact, Distancers usually blame their partners when they sour on a relationship, sometimes detailing frivolous complaints to rationalize why they do so. One patient told me he was ending a relationship because his fiancée was too dependent on her mother and girlfriends. Another announced that while she loved the man she was living with, she could never spend a lifetime with someone who was so politically conservative. Still another felt that the woman he'd been dating was "too quiet." Distancers don't understand that they're keeping themselves gridlocked by their anxiety, their fears, and their inability to acknowledge a pattern of expecting too much and therefore finding too little. By consistently zeroing in on what their mate lacks and ignoring the positive things they gain from the relationship—a feeling of being valued, respected, and loved—they keep the spotlight off their own insecurities and handicaps.

Frequently ambitious and career-focused, Distancers derive tremendous status and self-esteem from their professional identity and fear that making room in their life for a mate means they'll have to relinquish some of that power. They are ruled by their Filofaxes and can always justify their busy calendars—"Go to the country this weekend? That big project is due. I have to go to the office." ... "Of course I want to be with you, but if I'm going to make partner, I can't leave early when every other associate is there until ten P.M." In truth, their devotion to their work is a convenient excuse for not being emotionally and physically present.

Paradoxically, once the Distancer finds the space he thinks he needs, he feels empty and lonely and convinces himself all over again that he wants to be close. But as soon as he reconnects with a lover or finds a new partner, he starts looking around for the exit—just in case. In the short term, exiting a relationship does make the Distancer feel less anxious. But it's a momentary reprieve, short-term relief in exchange for a long-term cost. The issues that aren't addressed, the needs that aren't processed always resurface in future relationships.

Like Dan, many Distancers use sex as a substitute for true intimacy. Inside the bedroom Dan feels competent and in charge. When he's making love, he believes he's being sensitive and attuned to his partner's needs. But take him outside the bedroom and into a situation that demands emotional maturity, and he's stumped. "How can we be this great in bed and have it not work out?" he asked me.

If you're gridlocked in the Distancer rut, being close makes you feel vulnerable, dependent, and suffocated. Perhaps you were badly burned by a past relationship or are fearful of replicating your parents' bad marriage. Riddled with self-doubt, you're terrified of making a mistake. The thought of sharing your life with someone—of revealing your fears and inadequacies as well as your strengths and your dreams—is stifling. If someone knows you well, you're convinced that he or she will ultimately reject you. Though you may even be aware on some level that you're holding yourself back because you're afraid of being hurt, you struggle with the question "Is it him or is it me?" You're not sure if your concerns are valid or if you're simply being too picky. Rather than risk the pain of being left, you do the leaving yourself.

STOPLIGHT: THE FEAR OF INTIMACY

Ambivalence is both the hallmark of a Distancer's behavior and the trigger for it, holding him back from making a lasting commitment. That's because Distancers are programmed early on to distrust any intimate relationship. A Distancer's parents might have been smothering and intrusive, or critical and uninvolved. In either case a child learns that the only way to shield himself from being misunderstood or manipulated is to build a wall around his heart and strive to be independent, so he isn't disappointed by depending on someone who doesn't follow through for him. Distancers want to be close, but at the same time they need to pull away. Any long-term involvement is difficult for them, if not impossible.

Dan's family, for example, was saturated with stress and worry. Preoccupied with their own problems, his parents had little time and even less emotional energy for their youngest son. His father, a salesman who made money but managed it poorly, was rarely home, and when he was, he was either out with his cronies or buried behind the newspaper. His mother, tense and bitter, complained relentlessly about his father's irresponsibility. "They were always arguing," Dan told me. Dan tried to fill his father's shoes as best he could, giving up weekends to run errands for his mother and even do the home repairs for which his father never found the time.

"They weren't mean or abusive, and I know they loved me, but I honestly can't remember one instance when Mom came to a baseball or basketball game I played in, one time that Dad helped me with homework when I couldn't figure it out. The only time I got noticed," Dan said with more than a trace of sadness, "is when I did something wrong. Then I'd hear about it for sure." Dan tried to be a good boy. "I didn't want to give my mom anything else to worry about," he added. Since Distancers like Dan were made to feel that their interests and hopes were a burden, they'd forfeit or minimize them. "When I was in sixth grade, I was passionate about ice hockey," he recalled. "All my friends were trying out for the team, but I knew my folks would never be able to afford all that expensive equipment. I didn't need to ask. I just knew."

Because Dan's parents had never been there for him in a consistently nurturing way, he didn't know what it meant to rely on another person. Instead, he kept his needs to himself, minimizing and even negating them. What's more, he had no role model for a happy, healthy relationship, and as a result he doesn't know how to respond appropriately when people try to show that they care about him. Self-sufficient, he takes pride in the fact that he's not beholden to anyone. Now, being isolated and disconnected from others is a feeling he may not like, but at least it's familiar.

Those whose past relationships ended badly frequently carry a residue of mistrust, fear, and self-doubt that leaves them gun-shy and throws them into a Distancer rut. That's what happened to thirty-year-old Kate, a management consultant specializing in emerging Internet companies. Divorced for two years from a man who had cheated on her during their brief marriage, she'd been dating Kevin, a banker who clearly adored her, for almost a year when she abruptly decided to move to the West Coast. "My family lives in California," she explained, "and the job opportunities are so much richer in the Bay Area than they are in New York. Also, as much as Kevin says he loves me, I'm afraid he'll never commit to marriage." Kate was astonished that Kevin didn't understand her reasons for moving, and deeply hurt when he told her he wanted to start seeing other women. She quickly blamed him for being unsupportive and uncaring.

Kate's reaction is typical of the Distancer. The older of two daughters, she had learned from her critical, overbearing mother and her punitive father that the way to win approval was to say what others want to hear and ignore her own voice. She had done that in her first marriage, only to have her husband betray her, an experience that left her deeply mistrustful of men. To give up a professional opportunity on the chance that Kevin would decide to marry was too great a risk.

Instead, she went where she felt recognized, appreciated, and fully in control of her life—the professional arena. To give that up, even for love, was impossible.

Talented, successful, and accomplished in work, Kate is one of the walking wounded in love. While she claims she wants to deepen her relationship with Kevin, she believes that Kevin's desire to date others is a sure sign of his lack of commitment to her. However, she doesn't recognize the role she's played in keeping the relationship gridlocked by moving away in the first place.

YOU'RE GRIDLOCKED HERE IF . . .

- You're hooked on safety. You always go just so far in any relationship before you feel stifled and start looking for a way out.
- You're extremely mistrustful of others and can't believe that anyone will really be there for you.
- You're afraid to share. Compromise feels like a loss rather than a gain.
- You focus more on a partner's shortcomings than on your own fear of dependency and closeness.

LOVE RUT #4: BOUNCERS

"BUT I WANT THEM BOTH."

"I never thought I would have an affair," said Claire, the woman we met at the beginning of this chapter, when she called to make an appointment to see me. When Claire's youngest son was ten, she re-enrolled in law school, where she met Andrew, a divorced attorney who was teaching one of her seminar courses. Over lunch or a quick cup of coffee after class, Claire found herself confiding her unhappiness. "Andrew listened, he joked, he made suggestions, but he never pushed me," she said. "He became a trusted friend first—and I realized, oh, my God, I was in love with him.

"And I certainly never thought I'd *ever* be talking to a divorce lawyer," she continued. "But there's just no way my marriage is going to work. I've tried for years to get Doug to change, but he basically ignored me, or yessed me to death, and then did exactly what he wanted to do anyway. Until I met Andrew, I felt trapped. On one level I knew I was miserable with Doug, and I knew that other people had partners who were more loving and supportive, but I'd more or less accepted the way we were. I couldn't even imagine a different life. But with Andrew I feel cherished. The way he takes my face in his hands and says 'I love you, baby' makes me euphoric. It's the kind of delicious, romantic gesture that Doug would never think of in a million years.

"With him, I feel happy and in sync with the world," she added. "For a while I didn't even think about the consequences of my behavior. It was the memories of my time with Andrew that got me through the days. But after a year of deception I couldn't hide it from Doug any longer. When I told him, he broke down and swore he'd change. I can tell he's tried to be a better husband. But I can't just stop seeing Andrew and jump back into my marriage. 'Can't' is the wrong word—I don't want to. On the other hand, no matter what the experts say, I know a divorce is going to shatter my children's lives forever, and I can't do that to them either. So what do I do?"

Like Stallers, Bouncers are deeply unhappy that their needs are not being met. But unlike Stallers, they don't stay put. As Claire's story illustrates, the hallmark of Bouncers is that they've not only moved out of a relationship emotionally, they've become involved with someone new. In their vain attempt to honor their commitment to stay, knowing all the while that they must eventually choose, they become gridlocked. Riddled with self-doubt and mistrustful of their own judgment, people like Claire bounce between their spouse and their lover, between guilt and rationalization. They know they're heading into a skid, but they don't know which way to turn the wheel to avoid a crash. In fact, it's not unusual to find people who have been Stallers for a long time actually mobilize to make a change—and do so by becoming Bouncers.

Bouncers aren't hit-and-run lovers who indulge in one affair after another. Rather, they are so starved for attention, praise, and love in their current relationships that they feel forced to seek these things elsewhere. Perhaps at one time their partner did make them feel cherished and needed, but through the years—as the pressures of home and work responsibilities piled up—they lost that loving feeling. Or perhaps they never had it at all yet clung to the hope that someday they would. An affair is the proverbial wake-up call that forces Bouncers to reckon with what's missing in their marriage.

Stephanie, thirty-three, is a perfect example. Until she became involved with Evan, a man she met at work, she hadn't fully understood that the reason she was so unhappy in her four-year marriage to Stewart—indeed, the reason she had stalled over setting a wedding date for years—was because their sexual life, though good, was not fully satisfying. Like many people I see, Stephanie and Stewart had moved in together and had settled into a lifestyle that was fun and comfortable. "I knew he loved me, and I felt accepted and content," Stephanie recalled. "Everyone said we were a great couple, so I guess I assumed it, too. We'd been together for so long, it was hard to imagine that it wouldn't work out after all. In many ways Stewart had so many of the things I'd always looked for in a guy, I thought that the passion piece would come. It never did, but until I met Evan, it didn't hit me how much I missed it."

Although problems were long percolating in Stephanie's marriage, meeting Evan was the catalyst that propelled her out of the relationship. "I was used to a certain level of squabbling, but after I met Evan, I started to get really angry at the way Stewart basically ignored my ideas and made all sorts of arbitrary decisions for us as a couple," she added. "He assumed that I thought the same way he did, and his attitude was unbelievably overbearing. There were days I'd get so mad I couldn't even be in the apartment with him." Disputes that Stephanie might have overlooked in the past were too difficult for her to ignore now that Evan had entered her life. When she came to see me, she had already bounced out of the marriage and into a full-blown affair with Evan—which left her exhilarated one moment and ridden with guilt the next.

Still other Bouncers use another relationship to actually help them remain in an unhappy marriage. Like Stallers, there is much that these people value in their spouse and their life together; some intend to stay in a bad marriage until their kids are grown. "My marriage is like a business, and I'm committed to making this business run smoothly, at least until the boys are in college," Harold, a top executive at a national search firm, told me. Though shredded by guilt that he's been unfaithful—and terrified that someone will discover the truth—he's unwilling to make the final break and ask his wife for a divorce. "Nancy is a great mother, but that's all she's ever been interested in. Once the kids came, our sex life dwindled from once in a while to hardly ever. She's never been particularly interested in socializing either. She's shy and so totally focused on the kids, I honestly don't think she needs anyone else in her life or wants our lives to be any different. I'm very unhappy— but I never saw my dad after my parents divorced, and I'll be damned if I'm going to ruin my kids' lives the same way mine was."

Amy, a thirty-nine-year-old New York City–based executive in the music industry, has also made a conscious decision to stay in an unfulfilling marriage, though she's been having a passionate ten-year affair with Peter and doesn't intend to end it. Peter, who now lives in Miami, was Amy's first boyfriend after graduating from college, the man she left in order to wed Carl, an accountant, and the one she still turns to for romance, love, and support. "I married Carl because I thought that the life we'd lead would give me what I wanted," Amy explained. "Peter's a musician, and Carl makes more money in a year than he'll make in a lifetime. But it's all come at too high a price. Our marriage is a sham as far as the love aspect goes. It's based on practicalities— what works for the kids, really. It may look good on the surface—two successful people, two bright, delightful daughters. I doubt that any of our friends would ever guess that our relationship is in total meltdown. Carl and I just can't communicate on an emotional level, so we do our best to avoid each other. We hardly ever have sex, except on rare occasions, and even then it's perfunctory. Of course, I wish things were different. For a long time I tried not to dwell on it. But I never sense that my husband is excited to be with me. We both adore our kids, though, and want them to grow up in an intact home."

The only way Amy has been able to remain in a loveless, sexless marriage is because Peter is in her life. Four times a year, on the pretense of meeting with clients or attending a new musical opening, Amy flies to Miami to see Peter. Whenever she has a fight with Carl, she calls Peter. "I can't give him up. With Peter, I'm the 'me' I like. I just need to hear his voice. Then I feel better and know that I can handle the rest of my life."

Though the motivation for straying may be different for each Bouncer, the reaction is not. When Bouncers feel deprived, they get angry and then feel entitled to turn to someone else to give them what they need: power, independence, the feeling that they're cherished. Indeed, the Bouncer's anger is often so intense it obliterates any feelings of remorse; many feel so entitled to get what they don't have that they justify their behavior no matter how inappropriate and hurtful it is. "I don't think I'm doing anything wrong," one man defensively told his wife of fifteen years after he took his new girlfriend to spend the weekend at their beach house, a home the wife had lovingly furnished over the course of their marriage. "It's just as much my house as it is yours."

Though their partners may be oblivious to their brewing resentment, Bouncers have usually been waiting to leave for a long time. Unlike Stallers, who resign themselves to a bad situation and offset their ambivalence by trying even harder to please a partner, Bouncers may have coaxed, complained, pushed, and prodded to make relationship changes, but eventually they gave up. They stay in the marriage physically, but emotionally they step out and look to a lover to give them what they are missing. However, because they have stopped railing, a partner assumes they are content with the status quo—and is then astounded to learn the truth.

Some Bouncers actually seek out a new partner, but many more fall into a new romance unexpectedly, often at work. Jim, a sales representative, first came to see me because he and his wife Susan were unhappy with the lack of sex in their marriage. During our first meeting, Jim said, "She says it's my fault—that I don't spend enough time with her and that when I do, I always seem distracted and uninvolved." Jim finds it hard to reach into his soul and pull out his true feelings. Ask how his marriage has been all these years, and he'll say he believed it was "fine." "Susan's a little controlling, but my mother was, too, and we all learned to tune her out," he joked. In fact, Jim was proud of the fact that he and his wife rarely argued.

However, it soon became apparent that Jim's peacekeeping tactics were predicated on doing what Susan liked and wanted rather than on an exchange of ideas or any mutual decision-making. In truth, there had been no room for Jim in this marriage, yet he didn't realize that the long hours he felt compelled to put in at the office were his way of squeezing out more emotional space for himself.

Jim's needs were legitimate, but he still felt guilty having them. What's more, the way he sought to meet them was exacerbating the problems with Susan. "She's a lot more articulate than me," Jim said. "She knows precisely what she wants, and I don't care all that much, so I usually go along." In fact, Jim was as surprised as Susan when he fell in love with a colleague and expressed his pent-up rage at his wife by moving in with the other woman after only three months. At this point he knows he needs to be with his lover, and have time away from Susan, before he can make any final decision.

For Jim and Bouncers like him, the excitement and stimulation of working with someone on a project can trigger sexual desire as well. Brainstorming ideas, admiring a colleague's work, and sharing the adrenaline rush when a project finally succeeds becomes a kind of mental foreplay. It's thrilling to be with someone who listens, understands, and supports you, especially when your marriage is empty of all that.

STOPLIGHT: THE FEAR OF LOSS

Once again, past abandonments can resurface and gridlock people in the Bouncer rut. As soon as Bouncers feel deprived of passion, attention, and interest on the part of a partner, they are reminded of similar experiences they had with not-there parents who failed to meet their earliest needs. Indeed, Bouncers feel so empty and one-down that they are unable to tolerate loss of any kind, and they'll do everything they can to make sure they never have to.

At the same time, Bouncers have a low tolerance for the more mundane, occasionally frustrating aspects of marriage. The demands of juggling work and family, the pressures and worries of raising children, the boredom and weariness that inevitably strike every relationship further deplete the Bouncer and compound his feelings of rejection. To fill the void, the Bouncer seeks a new lover who will worship, praise, and support him.

However, once he finds what he thinks he's looking for, he often becomes gridlocked. The Bouncer simply cannot decide whether to stay or to leave. Saying yes to one and letting the other one go means that once again he must face a loss—an option akin to severing a vital part of his self-esteem. By taking a lover, Claire, Amy, Stephanie, and Jim are saying to their spouse, "I don't need to feel dependent on you or out of control in this marriage anymore." Like children who can never get enough love and attention from their parents, Bouncers use their infidelity to feel powerful.

For example, Claire comes from a politically prominent family and both of her parents were heavily involved in community activities. At home, appearances counted more than feelings. No one in Claire's family was ever allowed to disagree or get angry—anyone who ever did was quickly labeled selfish and thoughtless. As a result, Claire never felt she had permission to say what was really on her mind, and she silently accepted years of unhappiness until she met a man who knew how to listen. Similarly, Amy lost her mother when she was four and, though her father remarried, she never felt close to her stepmother. Her unhappy marriage feels perilously close to her unhappy childhood, and by stealing a few weekends of happiness with Peter, she's unconsciously attempting to reclaim the feeling of being cherished that she had before her mother died.

Jim also grew up in a home filled with another kind of deprivation. Conflict was strictly avoided, people never raised their voices and, if Jim felt resentful, he never acknowledged it to anyone, including himself. When he married Susan and settled in New York, he continued to submit quietly to her wishes and directions. Indeed, he taught her that this was the way he wanted their life to be. Susan, however, had grown up with a domineering father, and rather than shy away from a good fight, she learned to lay her feelings on the table and to give as good as she got. While Jim isn't sure about whether to end his marriage, being with his lover makes him realize how much more open, honest, and expressive he can be with his feelings. "I've just started to find the real me," he said. "Incredibly, I didn't know I was lost."

YOU'RE GRIDLOCKED HERE IF:

- You're hooked on the high. The excitement of being newly in love and having a fantasy lover fulfills your expectations, makes you realize that you don't want your future to be like your past.
- You're resigned to the fact that your relationship will never change, and without your lover to balance all the negatives in your marriage, you can't survive.
- You're torn between two lovers and can't trust your judgment to make a good choice.
- You use your anger and emptiness to alleviate your guilt and justify your infidelity.

UNLUCKY IN LOVE?

Recognizing the gridlock effect that these lovers can have on you—and why their power is so pervasive—is the first step in moving out of a love rut and toward more reciprocal romantic relationships.

The Fantasy Lover can do no wrong. He's the one you wish you had, the one you've been holding out for all these years, not the one you have. Since he possesses all the characteristics you've always been looking for or needing in a mate, it's not surprising that your current partner can't possibly measure up. The only problem is, this relationship will never pass a reality check.

The Smothering Lover wants to be your sun, moon, and stars. "Compromise" is not a word in his vocabulary; neither is individuality. Unless you do everything for or with him, you'll never be good enough. Possessive and controlling, he wants you available at all times and deeply resents any people or activities that come between you. Since your self-esteem is dependent on his love and approval, you're willing to work harder no matter how great his demands. Smothering lovers don't include you in their world but readily inhabit yours when it comes to friends and resources. They don't deliberately withhold affection, love, or support. They simply don't know how to give it.

The Neglectful Lover reminds you more than you want to admit of the not-there parents with whom you grew up. With the promise of getting the love you want, he manipulates you into giving more. But the relationship doesn't feel equal, and you are always giving far more than you're getting.

The Yo-yo Lover is torn between his strong desire to be independent and his equally powerful need to be taken care of. When he does connect with you, the feelings are intense. Inevitably, he gets cold feet: As soon as you step forward, he'll pull back. With such an on-again/off-again relationship, you never get a handle on where you stand.

The Ghost Lover haunts your life. He was your first love, or your greatest love, and you still can't get over losing him. The person you're currently with may be all that you've hoped for, but you can't see it because you're looking backward, not forward. A piece of your heart is stuck in the past.

CHAPTER FOUR

WORK RUTS

"I used to leap out of bed five minutes before the alarm because I was so excited to get to work," said Brooke, thirty-two, with a hollow laugh. A product manager with a worldwide advertising agency and the mother of a two-year-old daughter, Brooke had dreamed of following her father into the career he'd loved. After graduating from a prestigious journalism school, she worked her way up from pencil-sharpening assistant to midlevel manager, thriving on the long hours and nail-biting tension inherent in the business. "I loved everything about advertising—the energy of creating a new campaign, working with the business guys to understand the financial goals or the art department to sharpen the visual message. I couldn't get enough of work," she admitted. "I'd go to sleep thinking of copy lines."

But just before her thirtieth birthday, the clear career path Brooke had carefully plotted grew muddy. She received a plum offer at a competing company to work directly with Claudia, a woman who had a reputation as a brilliant strategist—and an arrogant bully. Brooke assumed she could handle Claudia, who would regularly stomp down the hall, waving Brooke's copy in her hand, to berate her in front of other staffers for not using proper punctuation marks. She thought nothing of calling Brooke at home late at night to discuss or bellow about her latest ideas. "The phone would ring at eleven P.M., and my heart would stop," Brooke recalled. "I knew it was her. And when I answered, she'd bark commands, not even bothering to say hello or make polite chitchat. I felt persecuted by this woman—yet unable to get away."

In one particularly galling meeting Claudia tore into one of Brooke's projects and called her a "blockhead" in front of the entire creative team. Tears stinging her eyes, Brooke vividly remembers wanting to bolt but feeling glued to her chair, barely able to croak out her apologetic reply. It wasn't the first time, or the last. "After one of those meetings I'd beat myself up for being such a wimp and allowing any human being to talk to me like that," Brooke said. Adding fuel to Brooke's simmering rage was the fact that she did more work than any other staff member, yet she never received the promotion or salary increases that Claudia promised.

Many times over the next four years Brooke vowed to leave a job that clearly had reached a dead end and often made her physically ill, but her attempts to network were admittedly halfhearted. After watching several colleagues downsized to the unemployment line, Brooke realized that the number of challenging jobs at her level was shrinking faster than she'd imagined and, she reasoned, with her husband, Sam, finishing his final year in business school, she couldn't very well jump ship just because she was unhappy.

Instead, she remained emotionally drained, angry, and stuck. "By Sunday afternoon this suffocating anxiety washes over me," she said. "I don't know how I'll get through each week. I'm not sleeping. I'm polishing off a box of Oreos in one sitting. I want to make a change—but I'm paralyzed. Me—the hotshot with all that drive and chutzpah. All I want to do is hibernate."

Why are legions of people, like Brooke, unhappy at work? Why do bright, ambitious men and women, who thought they knew where they were going professionally, wind up fed up, burned out, or derailed somewhere along the way, their confidence and self-esteem demolished? Especially disturbing is the growing evidence that many previously focused, committed professionals in their mid-twenties to mid-thirties—not the population typically associated with midlife crises—are now finding themselves gridlocked, reexamining their career-driven lives and reassessing priorities.

The answer in many cases is astonishingly simple. People like Brooke carry their emotional baggage from childhood right into the office—and along with it all their unmet needs, unfulfilled expectations, fears, and anxieties. Many experience their bosses as behaving and reacting like their mother or father, their colleagues like their siblings. As a result, they become embroiled in emotional conflicts that leave them feeling disappointed or simply burned out, not knowing what to do or which way to turn. Issues of dependence, independence, and control become triggered at work, creating ruts in which people become gridlocked as they try to pursue their goals of autonomy, self-satisfaction, and individuality.

Even the most accomplished and ambitious among them may be unaware that a range of very basic needs and expectations—the need for a strong sense of identity and self-worth, the need to be number one, the need to feel acknowledged, the need to be in control of their own lives—can make them vulnerable in the work setting. Women in particular, raised to be compassionate, cooperative, and empathic, expect that a job will give them personal gratification, recognition, and acknowledgment. Add to that the burden of being the perfect wife, mother, and career woman, and it's not hard to figure out why they're stuck. Often they operate with the expectation that their relationship with colleagues or bosses will be enough to protect and nourish them. Or they believe the mantra that if they try their hardest and do their best, they will succeed. They are unprepared for the seismic shifts of the last two decades that have changed the workplace terrain.

Some, like Brooke, may march confidently into a job, only to smash head-on into difficulties that seem insurmountable: controlling bosses, competitive colleagues, a sticky floor, or a glass ceiling. Working too hard for too little, they subsist on a daily diet of distress, frustration, and resentment. Even those who have attained a high level of success may still feel drained and unchallenged.

More important, the very real rewards they do derive from work—status, self-esteem, money—may in time no longer compensate for overwhelming feelings of emptiness, powerlessness, anxiety, guilt, and depression. Everything begins to feel out of whack, yet they can't figure out what's preventing them from deciding what they want to do. While there are myriad reasons people become stalled in dead-end jobs instead of focusing their energies to attain their goals, most are gridlocked in five key ruts.

WORK RUT #1: OVERDRIVERS

"I THOUGHT THIS WAS WHAT I WANTED TO DO, BUT I FEEL BORED AND UNCHALLENGED."

Thirty-two-year-old David, a psychologist, knew since he was sixteen that he wanted to work with children and teens, and ever since he graduated from college, he's been striving to meet that goal. Though he heads a mental-health program at a community clinic during the day, he also sees private patients before and after work and squeezes in classes for his doctorate whenever he can. Though his wife of two years urged him to slow down, David even took on a job as an adjunct professor teaching graduates. For several years he checked off each accomplishment according to plan.

"I've always been energized by my work," David told me. "I've never minded the long hours spent helping students shape their lives. But now I actually hate what I do. Instead of welcoming my students' questions and ideas, I resent their demands on my time and have no patience for their anxieties and hang-ups—which, of course, is precisely what a good teacher should have! The stress is really getting to me."

Recently David was offered an associate professorship—a coveted position, especially for someone so young—but he knows in his heart he doesn't want to take it. "My wife is pushing me to take it because it will place me on the tenure track, and I can see her point," he said. "The trouble is, I just don't know what I want anymore. I've always been so sure, so motivated. Now it's like I'm stuck in quicksand, and it's hard to decide. If I accept the university offer, I don't think it will be satisfying. Besides, I've worked so hard to build up my private practice, how can I put off my real dream of doing that just because everyone thinks a university spot is so ideal? Then again, going off on my own is a gamble. How do I know I'll make it? What if I can't support myself?"

Then there's Kim, thirty-three, a human-resources manager, who left a comfortable corporate job for the challenge of helping a small firm get off the ground. She knew the risks but thrived on the tension, challenge, and excitement that a start-up affords. Told by her boss that after three months she'd be able to hire a support staff, she gladly plunged into frantic eighteen-hour days. But it's been more than a year now, and Kim knows there's still no budget for a staff increase.

"This job is making me sick," she told me with a sigh of resignation. "I don't have time to eat, I hardly sleep. My husband, who was initially supportive, is now furious, and we're fighting all the time. He makes dinner, since he's always home before me. But though I tell him I'll get there by eight, the truth is, I never leave the office before nine-thirty every night. I know I can't continue like this, but I also know I can't leave. My boss depends on me. I promised to do this; I'll be a quitter if I don't." But Kim is so consumed with getting the job done that any enjoyment she used to glean from it has evaporated.

David and Kim are gridlocked in the Overdrive rut. Talented and ambitious, they've both carefully plotted their career paths until they reached precisely where they thought they wanted to be—only to wonder, Is this all there is? Though David has grown tired of what he's doing, he can't leave it behind. He's hesitant to try a solo direction because he's afraid to lose the security he has worked so hard to achieve. Kim's obstinacy in reaching her goal has blinded her to the fact that it may forever be out of her reach. Overdrivers do their job so well—staying late, coming in on weekends—that they frequently drown in the sheer volume of work they generate for themselves. Despite a take-charge exterior, a carefully calculated agenda, and obvious accomplishments, they feel so responsible for getting the job done that they do whatever they have to and work as hard as they have to, to make it happen. Sadly, any satisfaction they once derived from their job is lost in the grind of hard work, and they wind up feeling exploited. They long for personal fulfillment—a satisfying relationship, time to study or travel or simply to find themselves. But since Overdrivers believe they are indispensable to their job—or that their job is indispensable to their own emotional security—they are gridlocked by guilt if they even attempt to leave. Work is the focus of the Overdriver's life, and personal plans will always be shelved or changed at the last minute if a work problem arises.

When something at work goes awry, Overdrivers like David and Kim work even harder. They see each new project as an opportunity, something they really must do, and have a hard time saying no when something is offered to them, even though it might not be in their best interest. Unable to discriminate between when to say yes and when to say no, they wind up saying yes to everything. With their self-esteem based not just on how well but also how much they do, they can't possibly move forward. In their minds, there's simply too much in the way.

You're an Overdriver if you give to your job at the expense of your personal relationships, if you believe that any work on your desk must get done before you take any time for yourself. You may be one, too, if no matter how well you perform or how high you go, you still feel compelled to prove, to yourself and everyone else, that you're really good enough. Even though by any yardstick you've already attained many of your goals, in your eyes you're only as good as your latest success. In every endeavor you measure yourself by the outcome—a promotion, a salary increase, praise from the powers that be—rather than your experience of doing it. For you, the end is the only thing that justifies the means. But since you have such unrealistic expectations—leaving no room for missteps or setbacks along the way—you never get there.

You're also an Overdriver if, like David, you've become bored by work you used to love. You may realize that you're not happy, but for myriad reasons you can't figure out what else to do or how to steer yourself in another direction. Though you think often about initiating a move to reignite your enthusiasm, since any change might mean giving up hard-won professional status or financial security, you waffle. Just as you're about to make that phone call, rewrite that résumé, or start your own business, you hold back. The doing is daunting.

STOPLIGHT: FEAR OF FAILURE

For Overdrivers, praise is a double-edged sword: They are fueled equally by their need for approval and their fear of disapproval. For example, David and Kim drive themselves in order to feel competent and capable, and they look for signs of their success in the response of others. Since their self-worth stems from their professional role, failure triggers such feelings of inadequacy that they avoid it at all cost. Even making one mistake is not, in the Overdriver's mind, something from which he can learn. Rather, it's an indictment of his character, one that can leave him feeling ashamed and worthless.

David was raised by a devaluing father who dismissed his efforts and ridiculed his mistakes. Consequently, he dreaded making any and channeled his energies into succeeding at work. Doing well and moving up was the only way he could fill the void left by a father who simply didn't care and rarely showed his love or understanding of who his child really was. While Kim came from a family where academic success was highly prized, even as a little girl she felt compelled to work harder than she had to. Intense and highly organized, she often took charge of her younger sister and brother when her parents were at work, supervising homework and making dinner if they had to work late. She's continuing to micromanage everything at work as well.

On the other hand, some Overdrivers may have received so much praise for their accomplishments that they never learned to accept realistic limits or tolerate setbacks. When encouragement is overblown and effusive, children grow up to feel they can do no wrong. As a result, they may demand perfection in themselves and others. What's more, the overpraised child may also become so dependent on outside approval and feedback that she relies too heavily on other people's accolades. If she doesn't get them, the Overdriver becomes her own worst critic. Overdrivers have no ability to judge for themselves whether theirs was a job well done. Often anxious, they push themselves to do even better. Indeed, the compulsive Overdriver can't possibly ask a boss or colleague for help—she assumes that they're just as overloaded as she is. So the Overdriver feels compelled to do her job, and everyone else's, too. Kim, for example, even investigated a college course that promised to teach her how to function well on less sleep. It never occurred to her that she was doing far too much.

Still other Overdrivers came from homes where parents had particular expectations for their children, and failure to live up to them was met with criticism or, worse, no recognition or acknowledgment. Edie, a bright, articulate twenty-nine-year-old, had gone as far as she thought she could in a midsize stockbrokerage firm, and she was itching to start her own company. "I've put away a substantial nest egg," she told me. "I have the knowledge and the resources to do this, and I thought I had the guts, too. But I'm terrified. What if I'm wrong? I won't have anyone else to bounce my ideas off. I'll be the top dog—and uneasy is the head that wears a crown." As we spoke, it became apparent that Edie's parents, to whom she'd always been close, were less than encouraging about her new career plans.

"Mother tells me I should get married, which she's never said to me before and which I feel I have plenty of time to do. Dad sends me clippings from *Forbes* and *Fortune* to prove that I'm nuts to start my own firm. I'm beginning to think they're right. What if the business goes belly up? I lose all my savings—and with my luck, I probably won't be able to find a husband either."

Edie's parents had always supported her career choices, albeit with distant amusement, assuming that pursuing a career was something their daughter would do until she married and started a family. However, once it became clear that Edie was putting her job ahead of what they thought should be a priority in her life—settling down—they began to belittle her efforts. Unfortunately, their values continue to have a firm grip on Edie's confidence, heightening her fears and making her doubt her choices. "It's true," she added, "I know most of my girlfriends are getting married. And I do think about it. . . ." Despite her enthusiasm and obvious talent, Edie's resolve wavered. Three years later she's still working at the same brokerage firm—doing well financially, but aimless and disillusioned, struggling with the thought that she made a wrong choice, one she can never correct.

- Others dub you a workaholic—and you're not upset to hear it. You feel productive only when you're very busy.
- You have difficulty distinguishing between quality and quantity when it comes to your work.
- You believe you have to prove yourself repeatedly.
- You've reached your goal but are afraid to pursue the next reasonable step.

WORK RUT #2: BRAKERS

"IF I ONLY KNEW WHAT I WANTED TO DO."

Wendy, forty, a single mother of a fifteen-year-old daughter, became a nurse because that's what her mother and grandmother had been. "The women in our family were always nurses, and since I was small, I assumed—everybody assumed—that's what I'd be, too. I honestly don't remember if I ever questioned it," Wendy told me.

For the first ten years after she graduated from college, Wendy drew enormous satisfaction from her work. But in time her erratic work schedule, the rigid hospital rules, and the petty politicking—something she never thought she'd find in a healing profession—wore her down.

"I wasn't even enjoying being with patients anymore," she said. "I was desperate to make a change, but for the longest time I couldn't figure out what to do." Listless and depressed, she stewed for three more years before deciding to forsake nursing and join a friend in a start-up business selling allergy-free products. But sooner than she ever imagined—and despite the fact that her new business was thriving—the old feelings of ennui returned. "Whenever I think about work, I get depressed," she explained. "This job just doesn't feel like me. I'm a people person; I hate paperwork, and here I am pushing papers from one pile to another. It's so boring—but frankly, so is everything else I think about doing instead. Changing jobs again seems so monumental, I don't know where to begin. Now that my daughter is a teenager, I finally have the time to devote to me. But I haven't the foggiest idea what I'm interested in. Some days I think I'll take a course, other days I vow to return to nursing. But as soon as I focus on one thing, I find some reason it couldn't possibly work."

Wendy's a Braker. She sleepwalks through a job that seems purposeless, with no mission and even less passion for what she's doing. Brakers frequently believe that the positions they are in fail to tap their true abilities or talents, but they can't figure out what else to do. Instead of being motivated by their accomplishments, they find that their initial enthusiasm has withered. Rather than push to jump-start their waning interest, they continue to coast, feeling unproductive and unaccomplished. In the race to get ahead, they've placed themselves on the sidelines—permanently.

Not that it stops them from fretting about the future. Brakers worry a great deal, but they avoid making any real commitment because it just might be the wrong one. Pros at procrastinating, they're also poor time managers, unable to prioritize or determine which step is the best one for them to take next. They may, for example, wait so long to apply for a new position that they miss the deadline, then convince themselves the competition was so stiff that they never would have been considered anyway.

Some Brakers may unwittingly stall a promising career, even turning down a promotion, because it might mean they'll do better than— and wind up isolating themselves from—people they love and on whom they depend for support and morale-boosting. The Braker worries, If I make more money than my older sister—who was always considered the brainy one—will my family still love me? If I move up the corporate ladder, surpassing the friends I made when we were all freshly minted M.B.A.'s, will they still invite me to dinner and late-night, dish-the-boss sessions? If I leave the family business, won't everyone be angry and disappointed with me?

Jack admits that he slid into a job in his family's textile-manufacturing company because it was a safe, easy path. "I was always the black sheep of the family. I didn't know what I wanted to do, so I coasted through college and basically just had a good time." Now thirty, Jack wants to do more—and knows he's capable of it—but no one will take him seriously. "The only way I'm going to get a chance to test myself is if I leave and find another job," he told me. "But that's not so simple. I'll lose the financial security I have working for my dad. And I have to ask myself, Do I really want to kill myself? I know I have a very nice lifestyle; I have time to play tennis, see friends, do volunteer work. I'm not happy, but do I really want to give up everything else for the sake of my job? I'm not so sure."

While Brakers like Jack coast along in a personal comfort zone, others, like Jennifer, thirty-seven, an associate editor at a major national magazine, do so because they're uncomfortable in the spotlight. They convince themselves that someday opportunity will come knocking at their door. Jennifer was hired as an editorial assistant fresh out of college, and she gladly sharpened pencils, fetched coffee, and Xeroxed manuscripts for the privilege of working for one of the most legendary grandes dames of the magazine world.

"The office was like a sorority," Jennifer explained. "We all worked hard but also became incredibly close. I adored my job, adored my colleagues, adored my boss. I couldn't imagine working anywhere else." Over the years several other women who'd also joined the staff at the same time, or even after Jennifer, moved up. Jennifer, like many Brakers, stayed put, preferring to be a behind-the-scenes player than tackle the big decisions or shoulder the larger responsibilities that would be required if she moved up. Though friends encouraged her to push for a promotion, Jennifer couldn't bring herself to do it. She applied, and was rejected, for two jobs at competing magazines, but she never followed through with plans to consult a career counselor or try again.

Had the editor Jennifer loved working for not retired and been replaced by a successor hell-bent on clearing house, Jennifer would probably still be sitting in her same small cubicle. "With my seventeen-year track record under the old regime, the new editor-in-chief wasn't about to trust me or give me a chance," Jennifer recalled. "She hated everything I did, and I had no choice but to find another job— thank God." The spot she now has taps her creative talents and forced her to think: "If I hadn't been fired, I never would have grown. I never would have realized that there was more than one place where I could be happy, personally as well as professionally," she said.

If you're a Braker like Wendy, Jack, or Jennifer, you're quick to rationalize why you're staying put. Bound by family expectations of what you should do, you never stop to evaluate what you want to do. If you did, you might be forced to stand up for your values and needs in the face of others—risky business for Brakers who still haven't dealt sufficiently with basic separation and individuation issues. You remind yourself that your work hours are convenient, so you have more time to play golf or be with your children; that your salary, though not as high as you think it should be, is good enough; that people with whom you work are kind and supportive. There's always some very good reason you neglect to follow up on the job tip you heard about at the last sales conference. You're actually afraid of change and fearful of taking risks. Sometimes you avoid volunteering for new assignments or additional responsibilities; you're convinced you won't be able to handle them.

In fact, you probably drifted into this rut with little conscious choice about what you really wanted to do or where you wanted to do it. In some cases you may be able to make a job work for you. More often you tread water—bored, listless, numb—not miserable but certainly not happy.

Brakers slide easily into self-criticism. "I'm lazy," you secretly believe. "If only I pulled myself together, I could make something of my life." More often than you care to admit, even mild self-blame mushrooms into the conviction that you're really a loser. As Wendy ruefully said, "It's like I have a fatal flaw, or I'm missing some essential gene that everyone else has." Because they are so focused on themselves as frauds, Brakers fail to see that the real problem lies with others. Perhaps a boss really is a merciless bitch, perhaps catty co-workers are stealing ideas, or perhaps the work load is unrealistic. Brakers feel guilty that they aren't working hard enough, and they struggle with a Catch-22: If they go to the gym, take their children to the playground, or even do their laundry, they feel they're wasting time they ought to be devoting to furthering their careers. No matter which decision they make, they think it's the wrong one. Brakers can't shake the feeling that they're being irresponsible.

STOPLIGHT: FEAR OF SUCCESS

While Overdrivers are paralyzed by their fear of failure, Brakers are terrified by the prospect of success. They're convinced that anything they have managed to achieve was merely a fluke or a mix-up in the personnel department, and certainly not due to their abilities. They face each new assignment or project with the same trepidation they did the first one.

"I get nervous when someone compliments my work," confided Edie. "I often feel that I don't know what I'm talking about, and I wind up second-guessing myself. If I write a proposal suggesting how we could tackle a problem more efficiently, I'll feel proud and satisfied, but only for a short time. As soon as someone questions me, I'm sure they'll find out I really don't know what I'm talking about."

What's more, while Overdrivers repeatedly strive to prove themselves, Brakers are afraid they never can. Many are so competent they reaped the rewards and benefits of success at a young age. Now they're paralyzed with fear that they won't be able to repeat their earlier performance. Doubting their ability to sustain success, they often decide ahead of time that trying isn't worth the effort. With such a fundamental lack of self-worth, Brakers fall victim to the Impostor Syndrome. Any minute, they believe, their mask will be torn away, and people will see that they don't have what it takes to get where they're going, that they've been bluffing all along.

Though Brakers want to grow professionally, at the same time they prefer—indeed, look—to be taken care of by someone else. Each in his own way is still struggling to fill an emotional void from childhood—and often do by re-creating in the workplace a psychological scenario or dynamic that mimics one with which they wrestled in childhood. Jennifer, for example, was a lonely child whose father died when she was ten. Her mother, wrapped in her own grief, had little time or energy for her daughter. At work Jennifer found a phantom figure in her old boss as well as in the general office milieu that gave her all the nurturing, protection, and sense of belonging she had yearned for. The trouble was, by clinging to it for seventeen years, she never tested her ability to fly on her own.

While some Brakers come from families with strong expectations for their offspring, others have families where expectations were few or nonexistent, and the Braker's self-doubts and insecurities stem from this lack of early encouragement. If your parents, like Wendy's, never expected that you'd amount to anything, if you were often outshined by siblings who were smarter, prettier, or more athletic, you'll grow up feeling that the world is an overwhelming place, filled with challenges you're not capable of overcoming. If you were never taught things but still expected to know them, you may wind up feeling stupid. Then, too, if your accomplishments were ignored or belittled—say, you made the soccer team but your parents failed to come to a single game, or you won the lead in the class play but your workaholic father missed every performance—you absorbed the message that your efforts really didn't matter much. Why should you start trying now?

YOU'RE GRIDLOCKED HERE IF . . .

- You're afraid you'll never be good enough.
- You're afraid that friends or family will reject you if you do succeed.
- You're a harsh self-critic and you psych yourself out. You dwell on what you didn't do or should have done instead of what you can do.
- Since you're afraid you won't be able to achieve all that you want to do, you do nothing.

WORK RUT #3: OFFICE PERSONALIZERS

"NO ONE APPRECIATES WHAT I DO."

Brooke, the advertising executive we met at the beginning of this chapter, was gridlocked in the Office Personalizer rut. Like Overdrivers, Office Personalizers have too much to do and too little time to do it. Because they also have trouble saying no to other people's requests, they often do the work of two but don't believe they ever get the recognition or credit for their efforts that they think they deserve. In fact, they frequently run head-on into a rigid corporate hierarchy or an abusive, demanding boss and are left with the bitter feeling that their work environment is decidedly unfair and unsafe. Office Personalizers see others as slow-moving vehicles in their path, impossible to steer around.

Despite their constant attempts to protect themselves, Office Personalizers are regularly blindsided by backstabbing, competitive colleagues who steal their ideas, criticize their efforts, and garner the accolades the Office Personalizers believe should be showered on them.

Office Personalizers remain astonished by other people's undermining tactics—"How can they get away with it?"—and are convinced that if it weren't for these selfish, overbearing people, they wouldn't be so gridlocked.

Consequently, they try to meet unreasonable demands that often require them to reschedule their own doctor's appointments, give up lunch, miss exercise class, or set aside anything else they really should do for themselves. By such sacrifice, the Office Personalizer turns herself into the boss's right hand—important and indispensable but only because of her proximity to power. What's more, the Office Personalizer couldn't possibly be anywhere else: She's too afraid that a boss will get angry or find fault with her. Indeed, if something on the job does go wrong, Office Personalizers believe it's their fault and reflects their inadequacy.

Carrie, a custom-order coordinator for a home-furnishings company, has always taken it upon herself to proofread her boss's catalog copy before it shipped to the printer. Even though there was a team of copy editors hired to do precisely that task, she prided herself in being able to catch their mistakes. One time Carrie was rushing to meet her own deadline and didn't have time to sneak a peek at the last-minute change her boss had made in the Christmas mailing. No one else caught the thousand-dollar-plus error either, but when Carrie heard about it, she spun into panic mode.

"I was so worried," she recalled. "I knew my boss was going to be furious at me. Even though it wasn't my mistake, I started rehearsing what I'd say to her, since I hadn't double-checked in my usual way. Forget the fact that I'd been with the company seven years. I couldn't shake the feeling that this is the kind of thing that would completely jeopardize my credibility."

Courtney, thirty-one, a single woman who works for a small catering operation, is another Office Personalizer who feels she can't speak up when her boss continuously takes advantage of her.

"Joan, the owner, never gives me a moment's peace," Courtney said with a sigh. "If we're doing a job and the tablecloths and napkins are wrong, I'm the one who has to drive back and pick up the other color. If a party runs late and we have to stay until one A.M. to clean up, she lets Marianne, her other assistant, go home but never questions whether I'm able to stay late and then drive nine miles out of my way to take her home. I really love my job, but I'm tired of the way she assumes I'm available to do her bidding day or night. How come she never asks Marianne to cut the radishes into the tiny flowers? Why do I always do the menial work, while Marianne gets to sit in on planning meetings with clients?" The one time Courtney mustered the courage to ask if she could be included in more creative aspects of the job, Joan gave her the silent treatment for a week. "I learned my lesson," Courtney said. "If I want to keep my job, I better be the good little girl." Quitting and finding another position has never entered Courtney's mind. She feels helpless to defend herself, totally dependent on Joan for her livelihood and self-esteem, and continues to try to be indispensable to her.

Office Personalizers like Courtney have no strategies to get what they need and believe that their only modus operandi is to push even harder to gain the approval and favor of those who do them wrong. Rather than learn to assert their needs and set appropriate limits around inappropriate behavior or requests, they sink deeper into gridlock.

If you're an Office Personalizer like Brooke, Carrie, and Courtney, you arbitrarily jump to negative conclusions about yourself that bear little or no resemblance to reality. You are easily intimidated by a boss's or colleague's behavior, be it outright bullying or silent withdrawal. It just feels too threatening. Demoralized by your inability to break out of your rut, supersensitive and easily wounded by perceived slights, you feel defeated or belittled if a request for a more creative assignment is ignored, a phone call is not returned, or someone passes you in the hallway without a smile. Instead of thinking, "That person must be having a bad day," or "She's preoccupied with her own problems," you assume she doesn't think your work is up to par or that you're unworthy of her attention. Since you see others as strong and powerful, yourself as weak and powerless, you easily legitimize why you must keep quiet and stay put. You often listen to and try to solve the problems of others, but you confuse doing your job with trying to keep everyone around you happy. You derive your sense of importance from being needed by others.

STOPLIGHT: FEAR OF CONFRONTATION

Office Personalizers confuse confrontation with fighting. With self-esteem already shaky, they figure it's better to lie low than risk further wounds by standing up to someone in their way. After all, Office Personalizers worry, "What if they get angry at me? What if they retaliate in some way and make my job or my situation even more untenable?" If Office Personalizers were the target of, or witness to, highly critical, volatile exchanges when they were younger, any element of conflict or tension may be viewed as a sure sign that someone's gearing up to hurt them. To survive emotionally, they may decide that keeping a low profile is the best strategy.

It should come as no surprise that the fear of confrontation stems from childhood. Most of us, women especially, are rarely taught to express feelings in a healthy way. Whereas men who speak their mind are deemed assertive, women who do are considered bitchy. Good little girls, society still tells us, don't get even—it's not ladylike, and besides, no one will like you if you do.

The way sibling rivalry is handled can also influence a person's sense of security and fairness. Courtney, for example, had an overbearing mother who struggled to raise two children on her own and expected Courtney to take charge of the housework as well as care for her younger brother after school. "By the time my brother was eleven or twelve, he certainly could have done his share," Courtney said. "But the job chart had already been blocked out, so to speak. Mother treated John like a prince, and I felt like Cinderella before she went to the ball." Now, though Courtney may feel unfairly treated by her boss, she can no more speak up for her rights than she could explain to her mother she was favoring her brother years ago. After being told repeatedly that her complaints weren't valid, she learned to push those negative feelings away. But like all Office Personalizers, she still hopes someone will notice that she's drowning in work and throw her a life preserver. Meanwhile, a sense of futility and powerlessness simmers beneath the surface.

For example, Carrie's parents were high-strung and volatile, and she never knew when a conversation would disintegrate into an argument and they'd both lash out at her or her sister. She learned to keep her emotional antennae sharply tuned so she could anticipate any trouble. At the same time she tried hard to appease her older sister, by giving her toys or clothes or doing exactly what she was asked, in an attempt to align more closely with her. Carrie knew then, as she believes now, that take one misstep and she'd fall out of favor and lose her sister's affection. Instead of recognizing the boundaries that distinguish personal interactions from professional responsibilities, Carrie reacts with the same trepidation in both arenas. Office Personalizers like her don't understand that the working world isn't always fair and you don't always get the feedback you deserve. What's more, bad things happen to good people; bosses may be tyrannical or simply having a bad day. Personalizers see it all as a personal affront.

YOU'RE GRIDLOCKED HERE IF . . .

- When a problem crops up on the job, you think it's your fault. Others will be mad at you—or worse.
- You question other people's motives and believe they are deliberately trying to hold you back.
- Instead of setting limits around unreasonable demands, you try even harder to fulfill them.
- You often feel overpowered or outmaneuvered by bosses or colleagues. Work always feels unfair and unbalanced.

WORK RUT #4: SYSTEM SABOTEURS

"THEY SHOULD BE PAYING ATTENTION TO ME; I KNOW WHAT I'M TALKING ABOUT."

Maxine is the best first-grade teacher in the district—and she knows it. Confident and proud of her abilities to motivate the most recalcitrant learners, she's been teaching for fifteen years and has always been able to navigate the political potholes that cause many veteran teachers to burn out. But now Maxine has met her match. For the past year she's been engaged in a running battle with a principal who was brought in from another district.

"She's an idiot," Maxine fumed. "She may have a string of fancy degrees after her name, but she doesn't understand children. During our preschool conferences she announced that we were dropping the phonics approach to reading—which we've used since day one—and adopting a whole-language approach. Now, I use whole language in my classroom—we all do—and it can be a wonderful addition to the curriculum. But it doesn't work for every kid. Each child learns differently, and unless you give them every option available, you may lose a lot of smart kids along the way. But this woman has now banned phonics textbooks and tools and insists that only whole-language books be used. That's ridiculous. Of course, every one of my colleagues agrees with me, but I'm the only one who has the nerve to tell her so. They're all too afraid they'll lose their jobs."

Maxine is locked in a power struggle, one she senses she can't win, but that doesn't stop her from hammering her points home to anyone who will listen, especially Suzanne, a recently hired teacher and supporter of the whole-language-only reading method. Maxine was dumbstruck to discover that Suzanne, along with every one of her fellow teachers, had held a meeting and decided that Maxine had gone too far in speaking on their behalf.

"Because I'd been there the longest, they had initially asked me to speak to the principal. Apparently they've changed their minds, and they now think I'm a negative influence," she said, aghast. "Here I am, trying to fight for the kids, for what we all think is right, and they accuse me of throwing a monkey wrench into the system! I don't understand it." Resentful and disillusioned, Maxine felt ambushed on all sides. "I know they all call me a 'bitch on wheels' behind my back. Well, I think they're all dopes. They'd rather let this woman intimidate them than do what they know is the right thing."

Maxine represents one type of System Saboteur, and, like her counterparts, she doesn't realize she's her own worst enemy. System Saboteurs may be extremely capable, but they're unforgiving of anyone who doesn't meet their high standards. Convinced they know what's best, they are intolerant of failure—particularly in a person who holds a position of authority. Their motto, "It's my way or the highway," serves them well—until someone gets in their way. Since they have no skills for negotiating or compromising, and no social subtleties, they doom themselves to gridlock.

Thirty-eight-year-old Eric, an insurance executive, is another type of System Saboteur. Eric had always been the firm's rainmaker—tirelessly campaigning to bring in new clients and create better ways for his company to diversify. The boss's favorite, Eric spent his first ten years on the job in the spotlight of praise and admiration from those above and below him.

Enter Grace, a single woman who, in Eric's mind, became his chief rival. Anytime Grace made a new presentation, Eric was the first to point out its limitations. "We tried that two years ago," he'd say, pouting. "It didn't work then, so why should it work now?" Gone was the extroverted, optimistic young man who energized his staff. In his place was the company naysayer, who continued to do his job well—though he frequently arrived late or missed entirely the required Monday-morning meetings and sulked and withdrew from everyone in the office.

When he came to see me, Eric was depressed, angry, and confused. "Any day now I'm going to get the pink slip," he said, shaking his head. "I'm the best damn broker in that office, but they're all giving me a hard time. They're nuts. Okay, so I skipped the Monday meeting. Why should that be a reason to ignore my perfectly good comments?" Like other System Saboteurs, Eric resents being told what to do and sees no reason to play by other people's rules. What's more, he's actually surprised that his rising star combusted so quickly. Though he concedes that he can be negative, he believes that his colleagues should listen to him anyway.

Do you insist on calling the shots and making decisions, becoming enraged if your boss or colleagues ignore what you say or overrule you? Then you may be sabotaging your own chance at success. You're a System Saboteur like Maxine if you tend to say whatever's on your mind to whoever will listen, often confiding in people you don't know well and aren't sure you can trust simply because you're compelled to be heard. You're one, too, if you frequently find yourself blaming others for a perceived wrong. You're a System Saboteur like Eric if your calm, passive exterior masks a private fury. "No, of course I'm not angry," you may insist, though others complain of your sarcastic barbs. "I really admire the way you juggle your schedule to squeeze in time at the gym," one System Saboteur told a co-worker. "I couldn't possibly do that, since I'm frantically trying to get this issue out on time."

You may even start acting out your anger—showing up late for department meetings, failing to get a report in by deadline, or "forgetting" important messages. Outwardly or inwardly, you rebel at taking orders or acquiescing to others' suggestions. You don't realize that by working so hard to get and stay ahead, you push yourself even further behind.

STOPLIGHT: FEAR OF BEING CONTROLLED

Office Personalizers and System Saboteurs are close cousins. They both feel that their anger is justified. They are both rebels with a cause. The difference lies in the way they deal with and manage their anger. The Office Personalizer holds her anger inside, tries harder to please everyone, and dons the mantle of victimhood. System Saboteurs, on the other hand, vent their anger inappropriately, either verbally like Maxine or behaviorally like Eric.

System Saboteurs do themselves in by either their smoldering resentment or their unbridled explosions of rage, both of which blind them to the destructive effect of their words and actions. On some level most know that their behavior is out of control or at the very least ineffective. The trouble is, they have no idea how to put on the brakes. In fact, beneath their bravura lie intense feelings of worthlessness, which can trigger bouts of jealousy and envy that keep a System Saboteur gridlocked in power struggles, especially when he feels threatened. Even the mildest challenge may be seen by a Saboteur as an attempt to push him aside.

Some System Saboteurs may have grown up in families fractured by angry arguments, abusive behaviors, or even drug or alcohol addiction. They never felt that they could count on anyone to protect them. Many have never seen anyone resolve a conflict or disagreement without anger, and they have no idea how to do so themselves. Cooperation, aligning with others, working as a team toward compromise—these are foreign concepts. Their mottoes: "Do what you have to do" and "It's every man for himself."

System Saboteurs carry a big chip on their shoulders. Firmly believing they were wronged by what they experienced as children, they enter the work realm expecting to be treated as shabbily as they were in the past. They have their dukes up, determined that this time they won't be the powerless victim. However, with no actual experience about how a healthy and fair family functions, System Saboteurs can present their needs only in angry, blaming, alienating ways.

Eric, for instance, battled relentlessly with his bossy older sister, who tattled to their parents if he didn't follow her instructions. His parents had placed few rules or limits on either child, so when Eric and his sister misbehaved, no one ever said, in effect, "Enough. You've crossed the line." Then and now he continues to assume that his acting-out behavior is acceptable, and he's unable to see that he's shooting himself in the foot.

Maxine has a similar problem understanding boundaries and limits of behavior. Maxine's mother, she told me, rode roughshod over her dad and her two children, but Maxine was the only one who defied her, often trying to talk to her older sister and father and convince them of her mother's unfairness. More often than not they would turn around and align with her mother anyway, leaving Maxine to be the only squeaky wheel. She knew that she could never win, but she continued to try to get her mother to back down and apologize for her treatment of Maxine.

Interestingly, System Saboteurs may be responding to an overbearing parent with whom they were locked in perpetual clashes, like Maxine, or to a smothering one who always told them what to do and how to feel. Now every suggestion or directive makes them feel as threatened, helpless, and infantilized as they did years ago. They sensed it was pointless, unwise, or even dangerous to express their own opinions or choices; as a result, they never learned how to do it in an open, nonblaming, nonaccusatory way. Clashes with others are inevitable.

YOU'RE GRIDLOCKED HERE IF . . .

- You're so angry at being ignored that your judgment is faulty, and you find yourself confiding in people when you don't really know if you can trust them. You think you have an ally, only to discover that you're the only one on your team.
- You often feel out of control, like a car careening down the road with no driver.

- You wish you could change the way you react to others—but you never follow your own advice.
- You're the first person in the office to point out the boss's failings.

WORK RUT #5: CAREER MARTYRS

"IT'S MY ONLY OPTION."

Before she married George and took time off to raise her two sons, Stacy was a reporter for a large city newspaper. But after she'd stayed home for seven years, she and George bought a larger house, and Stacy realized she needed to go back to work to help offset the larger mortgage payments. The only spot she could find was writing public-relations copy for the chamber of commerce and other local businesses.

"I guess I should feel lucky," she said. "At least I'm working. So many others in this business are on the unemployment line. But I'm frustrated. I'm not doing what I was trained to do, and I'm wasting my education and my talents. I also know that the longer I stay here, the harder it will be to convince some editor that I really am a good reporter." Resigned to a dead-end job, Stacy has stopped looking entirely.

Stacy is a Career Martyr, and like all martyrs, she's convinced that her fate is simply not in her own hands. Myriad external circumstances—health problems, financial constraints, parenting obligations, a spouse who believes a woman's place is really at home—gridlock Career Martyrs and prevent them from returning to school to finish their degree, asking for a promotion, or taking whatever steps they know they should be taking to achieve the work satisfaction they deserve.

Working-mother guilt also gridlocks Career Martyrs. Kathleen slipped into this rut for years. Though she'd always dreamed of being a doctor, she dutifully postponed medical school, first to put her husband, Adam, through law school, then to raise two children. With both youngsters in middle school, it was her turn, and at thirty-six she was accepted and planned to enroll for the fall term. But then Adam received a big promotion—which eased the family's financial concerns but also required considerable international travel.

"We'd had a deal," Kathleen explained. "Adam was going to be the available parent, since we knew med school was a huge time commitment. He promised to be there if the school nurse called, to monitor the homework scene at night—basically to be Mr. Mom if necessary. But how could I expect him to turn down such a phenomenal opportunity? And I couldn't possibly be away from home as much as I needed to be if he was an ocean away for two weeks out of the month." Needless to say, Kathleen put off her dream—again.

Obligations to parents, coupled with a deep-seated feeling that they must do the right thing, also gridlock Career Martyrs in work situations that leave them frustrated and unhappy. Forty-six-year-old Ross, the father of four, never wanted to work with his father in the family's accessories business, but as the only son with a talent for finance, he was the logical choice. The company's thriving, but Ross is not happy.

"I'd really like to be an entrepreneur, putting small companies together with the right investors. I've told my dad at different points that I want to leave, but there was always some deal pending, and it wasn't the right time. I tell myself just to accept what I have, that it provides a good living. But the truth is, I feel too guilty leaving my father now, especially since he's nearing retirement age. Maybe then I can think about doing something different. After all, I'm not a kid anymore. I have responsibilities here." On other days Ross becomes depressed and lethargic. "What a waste," he thinks. "I'm almost fifty, and I'm still not doing what I want to do."

If you're a Career Martyr like Stacy, Kathleen, or Ross, you can't say no, especially to those you love. Bound by a sense of duty, you're unable to balance what you should do with what you want to do. You turn somersaults to please your children, your spouse, or your parents. If you begin to make a wise career move—say, to take a night class— instead of buckling down and studying, you quit before the third class. After all, your son just made the high-school hockey team, and *someone* has to drive him to late practices. Instead of figuring out alternative ways for him to get there—arranging for a car pool or a coach to pick him up—you abandon your plans entirely. Your job as a parent takes precedence over exploring any other options. Any move in your own direction leaves you feeling guilty that you're abandoning someone else.

Indeed, the life of a Career Martyr is ruled by a long list of "shoulds": You carry the responsibility for everything and everyone on your shoulders, even when it doesn't belong to you. As a result, you're swamped with regrets about what your life could/should/would be like if only the circumstances were different. Ironically, Career Martyrs don't realize that not only do they have a right to make a change, they also have the power to do it. Sadly, they feel like a passenger in the car, with no say about where they're going or how fast they'll get there.

STOPLIGHT: FEAR OF REJECTION

Career Martyrs are gridlocked by the overwhelming fear that if they stop doing for and giving to others, if they set appropriate limits and put themselves first, then the people they love will abandon them. They can't even tolerate knowing that those they love disapprove of their actions or plans. Many Career Martyrs were what is known as par-entified children—that is, they grew up feeling overly responsible for parents or siblings, perceiving perhaps that they were being neglected or mistreated by an absentee or unfaithful spouse or an abusive, alco-holic, or career-driven parent. Even now they may find it hard to shake such a profound sense of duty, and they feel greedy, uncaring, and irre-sponsible if they put their own needs ahead of others'. Career Martyrs confuse selfishness with selflessness.

Career Martyrs may also be so locked in by the norms and values set by family or society in general that they can't turn their wheels in an-other direction. Ross saw his grandparents and parents sacrifice to keep their business afloat. How could he turn down the legacy? Stacy and Kathleen, on the other hand, were gridlocked by traditional sex roles and expectations. Both saw their mothers put aside career aspirations to raise a family. Now, no matter how many years they've spent juggling home and career, they cannot banish the cosmic guilt that they're hurt-ing their children by furthering their own careers. What's more, there's always someone or something that can trigger it: the school play you have to miss because you're scheduled to be at a sales conference, the fact that your son has a learning disability and you can't possibly start a new job when you have to focus your energies on helping him with his schoolwork, the disapproving tone in your neighbor's voice when you mention something about your job, even a boss or colleague who drops not-so-subtle hints that if you're trying to be a solid professional and a good mother, you're probably not doing either job very well.

YOU'RE GRIDLOCKED HERE IF . . .

- You want to be an actor, a teacher, a doctor—anything other than what you are—but countless reasons, all of them valid, hold you back.
- You set a deadline for pursuing your career goal and fail to meet it each time. So you set another.
- Sacrifice is your byword. You can't compromise or see options. For you, it's all or nothing.
- You feel guilty putting your work needs first and worry that others will think you're selfish.

WORK-RUT SNAPSHOTS

OVERDRIVERS speed through life, afraid to slow down because they're convinced they'll never get where they need to go.

BRAKERS force themselves to slow down; they think they can't keep up with the flow of traffic, so they bear to the right and scan for the nearest exit.

OFFICE PERSONALIZERS never use blinkers to change lanes. Either they're swerving into someone else's way or discovering too late that someone has just crashed into theirs.

SYSTEM SABOTEURS have difficulty negotiating crowded highways and find it impossible to yield in the face of oncoming cars.

CAREER MARTYRS are perpetually gridlocked at the four-way stop sign, unable to move until everyone else has gone first.

CHAPTER FIVE

LIFE RUTS

Until now I've focused on how and why you become gridlocked in hurtful, self-defeating relationships with people who play pivotal roles in your life. But what about the times you feel inexplicably gridlocked with friends; in-laws; child-care givers; neighbors; professionals such as doctors, lawyers, and therapists; or even—admit it—personal trainers and hairstylists—people you know are not critical to your existence yet so often seem to be? If they consistently treat you with disregard, disdain, or hostility, why can't you break free from them? Most people can understand, rationalize, and excuse their stoically stuck behavior if their marriage or livelihood is at stake. But to put themselves in a position of constantly fending off the slings and arrows shot by hordes of others far less significant seems infuriatingly ridiculous.

Yet rare are the people who aren't, at some time, gridlocked in precisely these situations—confounded, demoralized, burned out, and self-critical because they're stuck in a relationship they may even know is toxic to their emotional well-being. Yet they feel compelled to maintain an unsatisfying relationship, because to end it feels awkward, harsh, cruel, or perhaps even more frightening than continuing the ordeal itself. There's Diane, the production manager at a Web site and mother of two, who is so dependent on her nanny that she allows the nanny to upbraid her in front of her children and agrees to the most outrageous demands for raises and extended vacations to ensure that she doesn't quit. Or Rachel, a savvy corporate lawyer who for fifteen years has willed herself to bite her tongue in the face of her sister-in-law's derogatory comments and wounding actions. Or Barbara, the producer in Chapter 1, who has become a doormat for her well-connected cousin Lisa, forever hopeful that one day Lisa will offer her an opportunity to get her dance company off the ground. In fact, as you may already have discovered, any long-standing personal relationship holds gridlock potential. What's more, being stuck in a rut with a friend or anyone else is similar in many ways to being gridlocked in love or in work. We just don't expect that we will be.

Indeed, most of us assume that the people who care about us will have our best interests at heart. We rightly believe that someone in our extended support network—certainly someone whose services we pay for—will, too. When it seems as if they don't, we vow to make a change: to tell a friend who consistently breaks dates or undermines our confidence that we don't want to see her anymore, to say no when asked (again) to baby-sit a friend's puppy while she spends the weekend at a romantic country inn with her boyfriend, to fire the nanny and hire someone new, or to find another internist who treats us respectfully and doesn't sentence us to hours-long waits prior to each appointment. Too often, however, our anxiety, fear, guilt, or anger leaves us too deflated to persevere with our intentions. Too often the pain of a splintered relationship leaves us as bereft as a love affair gone awry.

How can such apparently disparate relationships trigger such emotional upheaval? Once again, how you act and react to others is largely determined by the early conflicts and experiences you had with parents or siblings. Whether mirrored in present-day struggles or played out in phantom-figure relationships with friends and others, these early imprints continue to exert an invisible, yet powerful, hold on you. And while you want to believe that you've matured and cast off the old, childish ways of relating to people and situations, their influence can still leave you as emotionally gridlocked as you were years ago.

Any child can testify to the importance of social connections outside the family. Haunting memories of standing alone on the playground, being the last one picked for a school team, or finding yourself the only one not invited to a birthday party—all these are acute reminders of how closely our self-image is linked to our social success. Friends help us find ourselves and define ourselves. They help us reaffirm our self-worth when circumstances—loss of a job, the souring of a love affair—challenge our competence and attractiveness. The process of understanding who we are and where we stand in the world, which begins in our family of origin, continues with friends and others over the course of our lives. Yet unlike the spheres of love and work, in friendships we have no rules. Rather, we all carry within ourselves our own guidelines of what it means to be a friend, as well as what we need from those we call a friend. Inherent in that definition is the expectation that friendship will be easy and fun, that a friend will make us feel loved and accepted. But if expectations clash with reality—if instead of feeling good about ourselves when we're with someone, we feel insecure, rejected, or intimidated—we hit gridlock. Here are some of the life ruts that most often keep people stuck.

LIFE RUT #1: SERIAL PLEASERS

"NO MATTER WHAT I DO, IT'S NEVER ENOUGH."

"Can you divorce a friend?" wondered Patsy, the thirty-five-year-old graphic artist we first met in Chapter 3, only half in jest. "Kerry and I have known each other for ten years—we met through mutual friends, and we clicked immediately. She was bright, funny, and fun to be around, and she was always there for me. I'll never forget the night I was distraught when I broke up with my boyfriend. Without my asking, she came right over, listened sympathetically, cajoled me out of my funk, then made me get dressed and took me dancing. I could always count on her—and the feeling was mutual. I was as good a friend to her as she was to me.

But after Kerry married and had a child, the relationship between the two women slowly began to change. "Kerry became increasingly unavailable," Patsy remembered. "She and her husband weren't getting along, and she was so wrapped up in her own problems she couldn't focus on anyone else. She was never free to discuss my life, my job, or my family, only hers, and she routinely canceled plans at the last minute and refused to take my calls or call me back. Yet she demanded that I be as available to her when she needed me as ever. I started to feel used, but at the same time thought I should try to be a good friend." The tension between the two culminated in a nasty fight six months ago, when Patsy told Kerry that because of an important work conflict, she couldn't attend Kerry's son Max's fifth birthday party.

"Understand, when this child was born, I threw Kerry an elaborate baby shower and became Max's de facto aunt—an honor I took seriously," Patsy reported. "Whenever I could, I dropped by to see him. I never forgot a birthday, Valentine's Day, or Christmas, and I went out of my way to schedule business trips around any major events in Max's life. But this time I had a huge project to complete for work, and I felt a promotion was riding on its success. When I told Kerry about it, she actually slammed the phone down on me. I was dumbfounded."

Assuming that her friend was simply in a bad mood, Patsy let the incident drop, only to be blindsided again by Kerry's increasingly combative tone and lectures that Patsy wasn't doing enough or caring as much as she used to. Patiently, Patsy would explain and apologize, but Kerry was never satisfied. " 'How could you be like this?' she'd say. 'You're supposed to be my best friend.' " So Patsy continued to turn herself into a pretzel to please her friend. "I keep hoping that she'll snap out of it and be the old Kerry. To save my sanity, I try to keep my distance for a while. But sooner or later I relent. Why can't I make no mean no?"

While some people hit gridlock in only one area of their life, others—and Patsy is one of them—get stuck over and over again. As we saw in Chapter 3, Patsy is gridlocked in a love rut, but many of the same dynamics keep her gridlocked in life ruts, too. That's because Patsy is a Serial Pleaser. She assumes that over time her friend Kerry will be there for her just as she used to be. And when she's not, Patsy tries even harder to win her over, unable to accept the fact that unwavering love and support are simply not part of someone else's repertoire, and perhaps forever out of her reach.

A Serial Pleaser has very high expectations of herself as well as of everyone else in her life. She's most susceptible to gridlock during the honeymoon phase of a relationship—that period when friends first meet, revel in all that they share, and are often blind to character flaws and value differences that can trigger conflict later on. A Serial Pleaser refuses to admit that the friendship has changed and continues to yield to unreasonable demands, minimize snide remarks, and forgive competitive, unsupportive responses. A friend or confidante may downplay a Serial Pleaser's successes, ferret out problems she prefers to forget (or never knew she had), or shoot down her ideas with a condescending I-told-you-so attitude. But the Serial Pleaser, driven by an intense need for approval and priding herself on being a caring, loving person, doesn't know how to set limits no matter how insufferable this friend has become. Eventually she always gives in—emotionally depleted and feeling sucker-punched.

On some level the Serial Pleaser knows that what she's getting isn't, and never will be, equal to what she's giving. She also knows that many relationships leave her emotionally empty, but more often than not she blames herself for problems and disagreements, bouncing between trying to be understanding and knowing she should really break off the relationship. Like Patsy, she may even have attempted to do so. However, because the Serial Pleaser's self-esteem is irrevocably linked to making other people happy, she's soon swamped by guilt and always concludes that she has no choice but to stay gridlocked in relationships with those who are undermining her emotional well-being.

Samantha, thirty-three, an architect with a prestigious New York firm, is another Serial Pleaser, trapped in a painful relationship with her sister-in-law, Janice. "Janice was my grad-school roommate, and we were best friends from the moment we met," Samantha remembered. "We did everything together and everything for each other. We had the same sense of humor, and we even looked alike. If Janice was studying for an exam and didn't have the time to go to the library for a book she needed for class, I'd go out of my way to pick it up for her, because I believed she'd do the same for me. Janice was the one who fixed me up with her brother, Brian, and two years later we were married. I was so happy to help her I didn't realize how manipulative she really was."

But after graduation the first signs of strain appeared. "Janice had gotten married a few months before Brian and I did," said Samantha, "and instead of pursuing the law career she'd always talked about, she stopped working, moved to the suburbs, and started a family. Brian and I stayed in the city, and I started working at the firm I'm still with, eventually becoming a partner. But whenever I tried to talk to her about my job, she was cool and distant. There was an edge in her voice—as if she couldn't wait until I stopped talking so she could say something about herself, her kids, her volunteer work. I continued to show interest in what she was doing, but it wasn't reciprocated. In fact, over the years I can't remember one time that she ever asked me how my work was going, complimented my sons, or even thanked me for a gift. To this day she does things that are so beyond my comprehension—like inviting the whole extended family, second cousins even, for a holiday dinner and 'forgetting' to include us.

"It's funny," Samantha continued. "Though Janice adores my husband and insists that they've always been close, Brian thinks she's spoiled and selfish, and that the way she's treating us now is the way she's always been. I can't accept that. I still do everything I can to win her over, to let her know she holds a special place in my heart, and to make sure everyone appreciates her. Janice, for instance, never got along with her father, who adored me from the start. I praise and defend her right and left whenever he criticizes her."

Particularly baffling for Samantha is the fact that occasionally she and Janice do reconnect the way they once did. "At some family gatherings we'll slip into our old 'us' against 'them' mode," she reported. "But I never know which Janice I'm going to meet. Will it be the loving Janice I used to know or the catty Janice who can't walk into my house without making a petty or hostile comment?"

Over the years Samantha has tried to talk to her sister-in-law about their crumbling relationship. "Janice looks right through me, as if I'm talking a foreign language," she said. "Sometimes I'm tempted to be just as rotten to her as she is to me—but I don't like myself when I stoop to her level. And while I know it's crazy, in the back of my mind is the thought that maybe this time things will be like they used to be. So when she asks me to pick up a birthday cake for her daughter, since the bakery she loves is closer to my house than to hers, I jump in the car and go. She never returns the favor, but I do it anyway. Since we're family, I can't cut her from my life. But the truth is, she more than anyone has the power to make me suffer." Like all Serial Pleasers, Samantha knows that her friendship with Janice will never be the same. But she still keeps trying to turn back the clock.

One reason Samantha is gridlocked is that, like many Serial Pleasers, she's also a Serial Fixer, destined to solve everyone's problems. To atone for past or future transgressions, Samantha assumes she has to make everyone else feel better. You're a Serial Pleaser, too, if you're the person everyone turns to for favors or money, the one they count on to cancel plans and come to their rescue or listen endlessly to their trials and tribulations. You're also one if your need to commiserate falls on deaf ears, your phone calls don't get returned, and you think you're putting everyone else out if you ask for a favor or help in return.

STOPLIGHT: THE FEAR THAT YOU'RE NOT GOOD ENOUGH

Serial Pleasers are convinced that no matter how much they do, it's never enough or never good enough. Even as children, the harder they tried to win approval—from parents, siblings, teachers, coaches—the more elusive these endorsements became. In fact, a Serial Pleaser's yearning for understanding and connection is so strong that she willingly sacrifices her own time, energy, and needs—and tolerates incredibly hurtful behaviors—in order to get them. Like the driver who apologizes when someone else cuts into her lane and smashes into her car, the Serial Pleaser accepts all blame and responsibility. She doesn't realize that she's the one who just got hit.

The Serial Pleaser feels good about herself only when she sees acceptance reflected in someone else's eyes. Most Serial Pleasers grew up in families where demands, expectations, and criticism were plentiful and compliments, if given, were inevitably backhanded. As a result, their self-esteem became inexorably linked not to the kind of person they were but to what and how much they did for others. Then and now, pleasing and doing for someone else makes them feel capable and wanted.

However, after a lifetime of sacrifice, Serial Pleasers confuse their own needs with those of others. Incapable of gauging when they're giving too much, Serial Pleasers continue giving even more—and feel guilty when they don't. In fact, Serial Pleasers may become perennially gridlocked with those who in some way resemble the parent, brother, or sister who gave them the most difficulty growing up. Patsy's overbearing mother, for example, made her doubt her true feelings and second-guess her own judgment. Her friend Kerry is as critical and demanding as Mom. Similarly, Samantha's mother, perpetually busy with community and school affairs, was either too tired or too preoccupied to spend much time with her own daughter. Yet she insisted on constant attention herself and took great pride in her daughter's social standing. In fact, she focused so much on Samantha's appearance, academic success, and popularity that the little girl grew up to believe that striving to meet impossible expectations was the only way to make Mom happy and win her love. Samantha's emotionally distant father compounded her need, since he rarely offered even simple praise for a job well done. Now if Samantha lets one person down, even someone as hurtful as Janice, she feels she's failed. Janice's rejection leaves her defeated; despite Samantha's best efforts to please, she never can. Though she doesn't realize it, Samantha enters every new relationship with the hope of getting the recognition and affirmation that were either contingent on her selfless sacrificing—or simply unattainable.

YOU'RE GRIDLOCKED HERE IF . . .

- You're resentful of how much you give and how little you get from this relationship.
- Being friends with this person used to be fun; now it's work.
- It's hard for you to see that your needs are as valid as hers.
- Your threshold for tolerating disappointment is high.

LIFE RUT #2: BONDERS

"I THOUGHT WE'D ALWAYS BE FRIENDS."

Deirdre and Erin became best friends during their junior year in high school and stayed close throughout college. "Even though we were at different schools, we saw each other as often as possible," Deirdre, twenty-five, recounted. "Our phone bills were enormous. We shared everything—our feelings about our parents and our boyfriends, our dreams for the future, and, once we'd started working, even a pair of Manolo Blahnik shoes we both adored but couldn't afford to buy on our own." When Deirdre developed a huge crush on her boss, Erin was the one person she told. When Erin broke up with a longtime boyfriend, Deirdre was the only one who could console her. "I was flattered and thrilled that Erin was my friend," Deirdre continued. "She was like family to me, and vice versa. If my parents came to visit, we all went out to dinner. Her mother took me along on shopping trips as if I were her daughter, too."

But almost imperceptibly, the relationship began to tilt. Erin, increasingly frustrated in her entry-level job and no longer excited by New York's frantic pace, longed for a chance to live in another city. After a cousin's wedding in San Francisco, she announced that she was moving west. "Of course I was sad, but I was convinced we'd stay close," Deirdre said. "At least, I wanted to. But during that first year after she moved, it dawned on me that Erin didn't. I was always the one to call her, and when she came to New York to visit her family, she didn't even have time to meet me at Starbucks for a caffè latte. I'd leave these long messages on her answering machine, trying to figure out what I might have done to insult her, but she never called back. It was as if she'd erased me from her life just as soon as she erased the tape—and in the process, discarded a whole chunk of my life, too." Whenever Deirdre broached the subject of their disappearing friendship, Erin angrily denied that anything was wrong.

The final blow came when Deirdre told Erin she was scheduled for surgery to remove a benign cyst from her breast. "She didn't call or even send a card," Deirdre reported. "When I finally spoke to her a week later, I could hear the impatience in her voice as she pretended everything was fine but that she was just so busy and the time difference between the two coasts made it difficult to stay in touch." After a while Deirdre stopped calling. "I still don't understand why she stopped wanting to be my friend," she said. "What do I do now? Am I crazy to be upset? Or do I just step back and watch the friendship roll off a cliff?"

Andrea and Jody, twenty-nine, also became friends at a critical juncture in their lives: They had both enrolled in Lamaze class in preparation for the birth of their first child. "We were both in fashion merchandising, and our husbands were bankers," recalled Andrea. "We were both having girls, and we were planning on taking a number of years off from work to be home while our kids were young.

"Jody and I practically lived at each other's apartments," Andrea continued. "We'd pop over without calling, pick up groceries for each other, take our daughters shopping or to the library's reading hour. It was like a love affair. One call from Jody when I was feeling like the worst mother on the planet could banish my blues."

But by the time Andrea's daughter turned one, she'd begun to miss the challenges and adult conversation of the working world. As she wrestled with whether to call her old boss for an interview, she naturally turned to her closest friend as a sounding board.

"I'd always respected Jody's opinion, but it took me a long time to realize that she often pointed out the reasons I shouldn't start work again, not why I should. She said she was worried that I'd miss the most precious moments of my child's life. 'You have your whole life to work, but your daughter will only be two years old once,' she told me a hundred times. Or she'd remind me how the politics of the office used to make me crazy, and mention her friend or cousin who was juggling motherhood and career and hating every minute of it. Looking back, I see she really wasn't thinking about what was best for me. She must have felt threatened, worried about what she'd lose—our friendship, our times together—if I went back to work. She must have been torn, too, about returning to work herself, and she couldn't stand the idea that I'd made a decision when she was still floundering."

Indeed, when Andrea did start a part-time job, her friendship with Jody quickly soured, not with harsh words but with silence. "Jody has no time for me," Andrea told me. "Or time for my daughter either. She makes play dates with other children and tells me she never gets my messages. I'm torn between wanting to confront her and just forgetting the whole thing and moving on. But I want her to know that my going back to work has nothing to do with my feelings for her. And the truth is, I miss her. I miss what we had."

Deirdre and Andrea are gridlocked in the Bonder Rut. At pivotal points in their lives they each became so entwined with another person that when the relationship came unglued, it seemed as if they'd lost a core part of their own identity as well. As Deirdre and Andrea described, the Bonder Rut is characterized by intense mutual respect and admiration. Bonders often comment that their friendships feel like love affairs. They are impressed by a friend's abilities and accomplishments, excited by the similarities between them, and intrigued by their differences. Thrilled and flattered to have made such a powerful connection, Bonders don't simply *like* this special friend, they revere her, and they endow her and the relationship with such importance that they lose track of their instincts and good judgment.

The Bonder relationship may end abruptly, after a quarrel or clash of values, or barely perceptibly, as one or both of you develop new interests or connections and no longer share the same desire to maintain closeness. Whatever the case, you mourn. For when a Bonder's relationship dies, she loses a part of herself at the same time. "I'm not as tight with my college roommate, who's still single," admitted Sarah, a media planner with an advertising agency and a new mother. "I thought we'd always be best friends, but she doesn't want to tag along with me to the playground on weekends, and I don't blame her. I want to spend more time with her, but we're moving in different worlds now. Still, I miss her."

You're gridlocked in the Bonder Rut if you met this person during a critical point in your life. You may have had the same attitudes, behaviors, and mannerisms—even looked alike, dressed alike, and sounded alike—and you were flattered by, and thrived on, the similarities you shared. You held her opinions in great esteem and trusted her judgment completely. In fact, you found it hard to define yourself without somehow including her in the picture. Bonders feel genuine love and affection for each other, with no hints of jealousy or envy. However, while the Bonder relationship is initially one of mutual love, admiration, and support, once it begins to crumble, you feel sad and aimless. And if you're the one who does the leaving, you feel guilty and traitorous.

STOPLIGHT: FEAR OF LOSING A PART OF YOURSELF

Because the Bonder relationship is forged during a period of transition, uncertainty, or vulnerability, it can be extraordinarily powerful. A Bonder may be in the throes of adolescence, striking out for independence during the college years, juggling marriage and new motherhood, starting a new job, or wrestling with the searing loss—through separation, divorce, or even death—of a lover or spouse. To help navigate this uncertain terrain, she seeks a soul mate, perhaps someone who is going through (or has gone through) a similar situation, someone with whom she can identify and, in a psychological sense, merge. This person becomes an anchor in an emotional storm, a balm for a battered ego, the strength and security needed to carry on. A Bonder's relationship also mirrors her dreams of the person she'd like to be. The shy, studious college freshman will bond with her extroverted roommate in the hope that some of her social magic will rub off.

Just as the Bonder used to revere her omniscient parent or older sibling, now she idealizes her friend—identifying with her strengths, internalizing them, and making them her own. Through this intense connection, the Bonder feels powerful and capable. It is an experience much like the one a toddler has as it leaves a parent's side and ventures into the world, feeling safe because he perceives the parent's strength as his own. As an adult, you may assume that any friend you meet will naturally provide the same kind of devotion. Or if you were raised by well-intentioned but hovering parents, they may never have taught you that you can make mistakes, learn from them, and move on. Even now you may be too afraid to try to go it alone, because the risk of failure fills you with dread. Just as you looked to your parents for guidance and structure, you now look to others to give you direction and shore up your self-confidence.

On the other hand, if you feel that a parent or sibling failed to love or encourage you when you were young, as an adult you may unconsciously seek out in others the nurturing and acceptance you missed. The relationship of Wayne and Richard, two architects in their mid-thirties, shows clearly how Bonders find a phantom figure to gain the seal of approval they never felt they'd earned as children.

Friends since graduate school, Wayne and Richard saw each other regularly, planned camping and skiing trips together, played basketball, double dated, and eventually served as best man at each other's wedding. But in time Richard began to feel increasingly burdened by his friend's marital and work-related problems. "I know Wayne's marriage is not happy, and he's not landing the kind of commissions he hoped he would at this point in his career," explained Richard, thirty-seven. "I want to help, to be there for him like I always was. But it's just too much. He's a continuous misery machine, and I can't stand taking his long, late-night phone calls anymore. Besides, nothing I say makes a difference." Richard tried to put some distance between himself and his old friend, but each time Wayne called to meet for drinks or dinner, he reluctantly agreed. "I never have a good time. I'm always watching the clock and making excuses to cut the evening short. I probably should just say no when he asks me in the first place." Still, Richard feels sad. "I can't believe I have to come up with excuses to avoid spending time with him," he said, "but this friendship has become so difficult."

Richard doesn't understand that his reluctance to sever his connection to Wayne is due, at least in part, to the frustrating relationship he had with his brother, who was two years older and also named Wayne. Throughout their childhood, this brother, aloof and demanding, unloaded his household chores on Richard, was never appreciative of all the things Richard did for him, and frequently took his help for granted. Since Wayne had a younger brother with whom he'd never gotten along, their new friendship initially provided both men the support and camaraderie they had sought and never found with their siblings. However, in time Richard felt as unappreciated and burdened by his friend as he had for years with his brother. He hit gridlock.

As Richard discovered, when Bonders' friendships deteriorate, it feels as if a huge chunk of their life has been ripped out as well. Whether they are the one being left or the one who wants to do the leaving, Bonders experience grief, not just for the loss of a friend but for who they were when they were with that friend. After all, this was the person you dreamed and schemed with in high school, the one who stayed up late with you when you crammed for college exams, the park-bench mom forever linked in your mind with your children's nursery-school years. Losing the relationship can leave you gridlocked until you find a way to mend the hole in your heart.

YOU'RE GRIDLOCKED HERE IF . . .

- You've outgrown the friend. You don't like this person anymore, but you're not sure why.
- The only thing you share is your past—and perhaps a card at Christmas—yet letting go feels like losing a part of your own emotional history.
- You always thought of this person as "family," and the change in status of your relationship is awkward, uncomfortable, or painful.
- Whereas it used to be easy, it's become increasingly difficult to accept this person's limitations or his inability to accept who you are now.

LIFE RUT #3: EQUALIZERS

"I NEVER SAW HOW COMPETITIVE SHE REALLY WAS."

Friends for two years, Jill, thirty, and Holly, thirty-five, met when they were both on staff at a small magazine. "I was senior editor, and during a period of staff turnover, Holly was brought in as executive editor to help with the transition," Jill told me. "She was my boss, but we clicked in a way that's impossible to describe. We marveled at how much we had in common—both of our fathers had been in the magazine business, and—Daddy's girls—we followed in their footsteps. I adored her. She was brainy, witty, and had great personal style: Holly wore a man's fedora at a raffish angle, and she went with me to the store so I could buy one, too. Since our hair is the same color, and we wore it the same way, we joked that we were twins, and other people in the office called us that, too."

Despite the fact that Holly was technically Jill's boss, she treated her like a peer, marveling at her ideas and involving her in all her planning and hiring decisions. "Holly was an incredibly gifted, well-connected editor, but she never pulled rank," Jill said. "We'd work late every night, brainstorming story ideas, assigning articles, and editing each other's copy. We were both ambitious, but we could still laugh at the same things and appreciate the lifesaving qualities of a fabulous pair of boots." Jill looked forward to the weekends, when she and her husband joined Holly and her boyfriend for dinner at a trendy restaurant or spent time at Holly's cottage in rural Connecticut.

Despite their seamless working relationship, Jill still wanted to move to a larger magazine, where she felt she'd gain more experience. When Jill was hired as managing editor of a women's magazine, Holly seemed thrilled for her and even hosted a going-away party. But then she stopped calling.

"I'd leave messages with her secretary or on her home machine, but it was as if the woman had disappeared into thin air," Jill said. Then she heard through colleagues that Holly had been making negative comments about her and her work. "I was distraught," Jill confessed. "At first I didn't believe it. I was sure they had misheard the conversation. But when Holly snubbed me at a luncheon—and made me feel like a complete fool—I realized it was all true. I couldn't fathom why she would be so cruel. It was like Dr. Jekyll and Mr. Hyde. Suddenly I was seeing another side to Holly, one I'd never known about before." Jill couldn't see that her relationship with Holly had never truly been equal. Holly could be friends only as long as she felt she was in a one-up position. As soon as Jill won a promotion, in effect leveling the playing field, Holly's jealousy was so great that she had to break away.

Jill was stuck in the Equalizer Rut. Like the Bonder, the Equalizer begins a relationship reveling in that special connection, intimacy, safety, and sharing that serves to keep competitive feelings in check. However, while the Equalizer feels terrific about herself and her friendship, the relationship is seductive: Behind the façade of mutual admiration always lies some trigger that can unleash rivalrous feelings. Indeed, the Equalizer hits gridlock when a relationship that appeared free of jealousy or rivalry is suddenly revealed to be riddled with it.

Jill, for example, didn't realize, or refused to see, that under the seemingly placid surface of their relationship lurked a current of envy on Holly's part that wasn't apparent until Jill found a new job. Perhaps Holly wasn't aware of it either, or perhaps she hid it well. But once Jill was on a par with her in the publishing hierarchy, Holly must have found the situation so intolerable that she broke off the friendship, leaving Jill feeling baffled and betrayed.

Just about anything can trigger the rivalry that eventually sinks a relationship. A friend may be envious of your job, your marital status, your loving family, or even the color of your hair. For many women, marriage often creates the first friendship gap, having a baby the second. Single friends may resent another who becomes engaged, and feel left out, disappointed, or envious that they haven't yet tied the knot. Confidantes who are still undecided about when or whether to have a child may feel completely out of sync with a friend who has just given birth. Equalizers like Jill are oblivious to the competitive feelings of others. In fact, it never occurs to them that someone to whom they are so close would actually turn on them.

Annie, a thirty-six-year-old urban planner and mother of a preschool daughter, gets gridlocked over and over again in the Equalizer Rut. This time it was with a woman named Bonnie, whom she met when their daughters started nursery school. As their children's friendship deepened, the two women became fast friends, too, socializing with their husbands and sharing many weekends taking their daughters to the ballet and sledding and skating in Central Park.

Annie marveled at the fact that she could make such a true friend in her mid-thirties. "My relationship with Bonnie seemed as solid as the friendships I'd had with my sorority sisters in college," she recalled. The feeling appeared to be mutual: Bonnie always complimented Annie on her clothes or a new briefcase or on the way she juggled her work and family life, and frequently asked her opinion about children's programs, schools, or camps in the city. "I was flattered that she thought so highly of me, and I gladly gave her all the names and phone numbers of people I knew to talk to," said Annie.

At first Annie didn't mind that Bonnie would often buy many of the same things that she did, but it started to irk her when she realized that her friend would always go her one better. "One new suit I adored was an Armani knock-off. Bonnie loved it, too, and asked if she could buy it. Of course I said yes, but then she came back with the real thing!" she reported. "When I bought flatware—stainless, that is—Bonnie bought the same pattern in sterling."

Particularly disconcerting for Annie was the way Bonnie's actions triggered her own anxious, rivalrous feelings, exacerbated by the fact that Bonnie carried the competition into their daughters' relationships. "As soon as Bonnie discovered that my daughter had a play date with a new child, she'd rush to make a play date for her daughter with this child. But she wouldn't simply invite the other child to come to her house to play. She'd invite her to the *circus* or some other wonderful event. I know it's ludicrous—I'm embarrassed even to say it—but I started to worry that my kid wasn't going to be as popular as her kid." And though something about their friendship made Annie uneasy, Bonnie had a way of drawing her out, encouraging her to reveal her insecurities and worries, and making her believe, for a time at least, that she really did care about Annie.

"Being with Bonnie brings out the worst in me," Annie finally admitted. "I have to guard everything I tell her, because she always tries to one-up me. I can't share everything like I used to, because she takes credit for my ideas and acts as if they're her original thoughts. I feel I've been robbed! Yet I'm still drawn to her. I forget that she inevitably discredits or tries to trump me."

Equalizers go to great lengths to maintain the delicate balance of a friendship. Vicky, a freelance writer, gladly gave the names and phone numbers of editors she'd met over the years to her former college roommate, Liz, an artist who in recent years had decided to turn her energies to publishing. "I was happy to do it," Vicky said. "I'd been networking for ages, and I didn't think anything of it." Then Liz announced that through one of the leads Vicky had given her she'd had an offer to illustrate a parenting book from a major publisher and was looking for a co-author. "I'd love to bring you in on the project," Liz told Vicky, "but I don't want to be too pushy." Understandably, Equalizer Vicky felt threatened. Her friend had not only used her to get ahead, she'd cut her out.

Like Jill, Annie, and Vicky, every Equalizer I meet is astounded by her inability to see the manipulative or competitive qualities in a friend. That's because an Equalizer, drawn to the qualities she admires or wishes she herself had, is as blind as a new lover to another's character flaws or the deep value differences that can rupture a close relationship.

"Why didn't I see this coming?" Jill wondered. "How come I didn't know Holly was like that?" The answer: Most probably, those competitive qualities were there all along, and as life circumstances and situations changed, they rose to the surface.

Rivalrous feelings may be hard to see at first: the hesitation in a voice before giving a compliment ("I can't believe you're actually highlighting your hair!") or expressing joy at another's success, the slightly disparaging remark that minimizes accomplishments or discourages you from applying to graduate school to boost your credentials. Instead of rejoicing in the friendship and blossoming under its glow, the Equalizer begins to feel unsettled and diminished.

You're an Equalizer if a relationship you thought was based on a balance of love and caring now seems lopsided. Instead of feeling as if you and a friend are "in this together," you feel consumed by her. She may be copying your clothes, your mannerisms, the things you do, or the places you go, never asking permission and always trying to outdo you. Yet for reasons that anger and confuse you, you can't cut her out of your life.

STOPLIGHT: THE FEAR OF LOSING OUT

Even though the Equalizer doesn't think that she's in a rivalrous relationship, that's precisely why she's gridlocked. In fact, the Equalizer's intense need for unity and her expectations for the friendship blind her to the envious attributes of others—and cause her to stifle her own needs on the altar of the relationship.

Women in particular find it difficult to acknowledge and deal with competitive feelings. Unlike boys, little girls are taught to bridle jealousy or rivalry, to compromise and negotiate, even at the expense of their individuality. Nice-girl training has taught people like Jill and Annie that you just don't do that, and they both assume that a close friend will also be totally happy when something good happens to them, totally sympathetic when roadblocks are thrown in their path.

From where does this need for equality stem? As a child, the

Equalizer most likely experienced an intense bonding relationship with a key caregiver. The Equalizer might have been Mom's favorite or Daddy's girl. Birth order, gender, or the role she played in the family probably elicited unwarranted attention in the eyes of a sibling. If comparisons, real or imagined, were made, resentment and rivalry can run deep, and insecurities will be intensified. Additionally, if parents placed a premium on keeping things equal between their children in order to avoid any rivalry, the Equalizer will grow up, Pollyannaish, assuming that life and all its riches will always be shared openly and evenly.

Extroverted Annie, for instance, always believed that her status as Daddy's girl was balanced by the fact that Ellie, her shy younger sister, was Mom's favorite. She never considered that her sister might have been jealous of the special relationship that Annie had with their father. What's more, for as long as she can remember, she was called upon and expected to take care of her sister. When Ellie was homesick during her summers at camp, Annie was routinely called out of activities to cheer her up. Even in college Ellie found it difficult to decide which courses to take, and she regularly made pilgrimages to her sister's room to ask her advice. Since "share and share alike" was the buzzword in her family, Annie naïvely expects that each friend will feel precisely the same way. She continues to give and do for friends, just as she always did for her sister, and is stunned and hurt when they're unmasked as rivals.

The Equalizer is gridlocked first in recognizing that she must end a hurtful relationship, and then by her inability to figure out how to actually do it. Especially confusing for the Equalizer is that while she may be deeply offended by another's apparent disregard for her well-being, at the same time she may still admire many of the friend's qualities and want to remain close. The Equalizer's intense desire for the relationship to be the way she wants crashes smack into the reality that it never will.

YOU'RE GRIDLOCKED HERE IF . . .

- Each encounter leaves you feeling anxious and insecure.
- You sense that you need to be cautious about what you reveal to this person.

- Your competitive feelings are triggered because your self-esteem feels threatened.
- Because you want to maintain the friendship, you negate or excuse the rivalrous way she treats you.

LIFE RUT #4: CARE SEEKERS

"YOU KNOW WHAT'S BEST FOR ME."

As long as Caroline, her baby-sitter of five years, was happy, Diane, chief production manager at a Web site, was happy, too. But lately this thirty-two-year-old mother of Adam, five, and Tara, two, becomes sick to her stomach whenever the phone rings early in the morning. "I just know it's Caroline calling to say she won't be able to come in again," Diane told me. "I'm really upset. For the first year or so our relationship was better than perfect. Caroline started working for me the week after I brought Adam home from the hospital. I'd had a C-section, and she took care of the baby and me, too. She was my Mother Teresa. She's effervescent and charming and made friends with all the baby-sitters in the neighborhood. Caroline's one of the reasons my kids have so many play dates—even mothers enjoyed spending time with her. I know she adores my kids. Who could ask for more?"

Ironically, just as Diane began to feel they'd all settled into a comfortable routine, Caroline's attitude and attendance became erratic. "She's out at least once a month," explained Diane. "Either she has to get her driver's license renewed or she has a backache or she got her period and can't move. Like no other woman on earth works when she's menstruating, right? Any working mother will tell you that you're only as good as your child care. My world turns upside down if Caroline doesn't make it in, so I jump through hoops to make sure she does." Caroline, it seems, also has a temper, and her pride is easily hurt. "I've learned to be very careful about what I ask her to do and how I ask her to do it," Diane admitted. "I bend over backward to make sure she's not offended—and pay her handsomely to make sure she stays."

So much so that whatever Caroline wants, Caroline gets. "I'm starting to feel like a real dope," Diane conceded. "Caroline's salary—which includes generous medical benefits—is far greater than what most of the other caregivers make, and she takes vacation whenever she wants to, never when it's convenient for me. I scramble with a patchwork of baby-sitters until she returns." For the past few months Caroline has been taking Tara along to her physical-therapy appointments, often leaving the little girl with her sister, who lives nearby. "I'm not happy about it," Diane admitted, "but Caroline hurt her back, and if I don't let her do this, I know she'll leave."

Diane is gridlocked in the Care Seeker Rut. A Care Seeker entrusts others with her personal or professional well-being or image and depends on them to handle key aspects of her life. These people—let's call them Supporters—may care for her children or her aging parents. They may clean her home, cut her hair, sculpt her biceps, monitor her health, or manage her financial investments. However, Care Seekers sabotage themselves because they too easily allow Supporters to be privy to intimate knowledge of their personal dramas and dilemmas. Supporters may know more about a Care Seeker's difficulties with a backstabbing colleague, her never-ending quarrels with a boyfriend, or the way siblings one-up each other at every holiday dinner, than a dear friend.

What's more, because Supporters may indeed do so much, they become invaluable, and Care Seekers feel an overwhelming sense of obligation to them. Care Seekers and Supporters share a history and often work in such close proximity that the relationship takes on an intimacy that feels familial. That's why it's so hard for a Care Seeker to criticize or ultimately break off this potentially destructive relationship, despite the fact that a Supporter may be sapping time, money, and energy and, quite simply, doing a lousy job. Diane, for example, is so convinced that she cannot function without her nanny—and that her children's social lives will suffer, too—that she's willing to tolerate less-than-quality child care to keep Caroline happy.

This type of relationship usually starts out appropriately: A Care Seeker hires or consults with a nanny, therapist, secretary, personal trainer, agent, physician, or lawyer to do the things she doesn't have the time or skills to do herself. Depending on the relationship, Supporters may also become perennial ego-boosters, extolling the Care Seeker's virtues. Gradually, however, the boundaries in the relationship blur, the balance of power subtly shifts, and a role reversal takes place: The Care Seeker grows dependent on the Supporter, not just for her services but for what feels like her emotional survival. Afraid to hurt a Supporter's feelings, the Care Seeker refrains from expressing any doubts about her ability, in effect protecting a Supporter's self-esteem at the expense of her own. Compelled to squelch disappointments and maintain the status quo, the Care Seeker teeters toward gridlock.

Rob, who runs his own real-estate development company, has boxed himself into just such a corner. For years Rob placed his personal and business income taxes in the capable hands of his longtime golfing buddy. "I'm a Type-A kind of guy," Rob explained as he paced around my office. "I like to have my taxes totally done by the first of April so I have plenty of time to review them. For three consecutive years I've told him that, but it doesn't make a difference. We're complete opposites: He's the guy you see dashing through the airport at the last minute and barely making the plane, while I'm the one who gets my boarding pass two hours before the flight. His work habits drive me nuts, and I keep telling myself I have to find a new accountant. But every year I go back to Jerry anyway—and wind up enraged. I probably should fire him, but our wives are friendly, our kids are in the same class at school, and I know I'd feel like a traitor."

While misplaced loyalty is one hallmark of the Care Seeker, so, too, is simple inertia. Laura, a thirty-two-year-old paralegal, hits gridlock whenever she tries to tell her therapist that she wants to discuss ending treatment. Though she's been seeing the same woman for five years, Laura doesn't feel she's made much progress, and each week she swears she's going to find another counselor. She never does. "I just don't want to start all over again with someone new," she confided. "This doctor knows all about my family, my battles with my sister, and the difficulty I've always had with my mother. I can't see explaining all this stuff to someone else. It would take too much time. I don't have the psychic energy to do it."

If dealing with the proverbial devil you know is less frightening than worrying about the devil you're afraid you'll meet, you may be gridlocked in the Care Seeker rut. "I don't trust my manager," said Adrienne, a thirty-five-year-old actress who recently reconnected with her very first manager after taking a break from show business to raise her son. "I don't think Hank is doing as much for me as he could, and certainly nowhere near what he promised. He's told me time and again he was going to find me parts, but each time something mysteriously falls through, and I've reached the point that I can barely scrape together the rent money each month. I know he's helping other people more than he's helping me, and I suspect he's even using some of my contacts to do it. But he was the one who helped me snag my first Off-Off-Broadway role. He took a chance when no one else would even consider me. I feel indebted to him. So while I'm angry, I think I better just stay where I am. Besides, who's to say that someone else would care any more or try any harder for me?"

Like many Care Seekers, Adrienne insists that "sometime soon" she'll begin interviewing agents. "Now's just not the right moment," she explained. The trouble is, for Care Seekers, the right time never comes. Like Diane, Rob, and Laura, you're gridlocked here if you find it easier and often necessary to allow someone else to make decisions about what's best for you. You're stuck, too, if your sense of who you are and what you can do is so grounded in someone else's assistance that you don't believe you can manage without this person. If at times this person also makes you feel neglected, controlled, or taken advantage of; if you second-guess her repeatedly but feel like a naughty child for questioning her ability and advice, you're also a Care Seeker. "Caroline's like a member of the family," Diane tells everyone. "Fire her? Don't be ridiculous!"

STOPLIGHT: THE FEAR OF INSTABILITY

The Care Seeker Rut is particularly pernicious because it rests not on a feeling of well-being but on desperation, resignation, or guilt. Care Seekers are gridlocked because they believe they have no choice, or at least no good choice. Though they may complain and obsess about the way they are being manipulated by others, out of fear and insecurity—translated into misplaced loyalty—they do nothing substantial to change. Being steadfast and faithful makes everyone feel good about themselves. But Care Seekers wrongly believe they have to be loyal at all costs, accepting or excusing inferior work or hurtful actions and refusing to hold others accountable.

Any number of factors can be the catalyst for a Care Seeker's fear of instability and unwavering devotion. Early upheavals—illness, separation, divorce, or death—may have left a child feeling emotionally wobbly. The normal anxiety that everyone feels when change occurs or is imminent leaves Care Seekers particularly anxious; it's simply too reminiscent of the insecurity and pain they felt years ago. Care Seekers need to keep their external world intact in order to keep their internal world secure. Any change in the world as they know it—even changing hairdressers, agents, or therapists—leaves them feeling overwhelmed and ill equipped to begin anew and invest, yet again, the emotional energy needed to handle anything unfamiliar. For them, the fact that they are known—that is, that they share some history with a person, however unhappy or difficult that history may be—is more manageable, and potentially less disappointing, than dealing with what they don't know.

Some Care Seekers are also victims of bad parenting. Perhaps the mother or father was critical or inattentive, showing little interest in them and offering scant encouragement. They learned as children not to make waves, to be compliant, cooperative, and uncomplaining— grateful to anyone who offered them any attention at all. For example, Diane's father traveled frequently on business, and her depressed, unresponsive mother depended on Diane to care for her two younger sisters. When Diane did so willingly, Mother was happy. If she balked at the unrealistic burden her mother had placed on her, she was rebuked as selfish. She never learned to assert her own rights or care for her own needs. In fact, doing so even now makes her feel guilty. Care Seekers may recognize the neglectful behavior on the part of Supporters, but it feels similar to what they've known. A skewed sense of responsibility prevents them from looking out for themselves by making decisions that are in their own best interest.

Like Serial Pleasers, Care Seekers want others to like them. The difference is that the Care Seeker is gridlocked in a professional relationship where such feelings are inappropriate. However, since Care Seekers turn everyone into a close friend or member of the family, they blur the lines of responsibility and expectation and compromise their right to quality care. Your hairstylist doesn't have to love you. He just has to cut your hair well. The Care Seeker knows this intellectually— but she can't feel it emotionally.

YOU'RE GRIDLOCKED HERE IF . . .

- You feel an overwhelming sense of obligation to this person. You believe you owe him something, and you disregard the evidence that he isn't delivering what he's promised to.
- You're too timid to assert your needs and take charge.
- You rely on others to know what's best for you.
- You experience a role reversal: In your mind, this person is the all-knowing parent and you're the child whose job it is to listen and obey.

PART TWO

BREAKING FREE

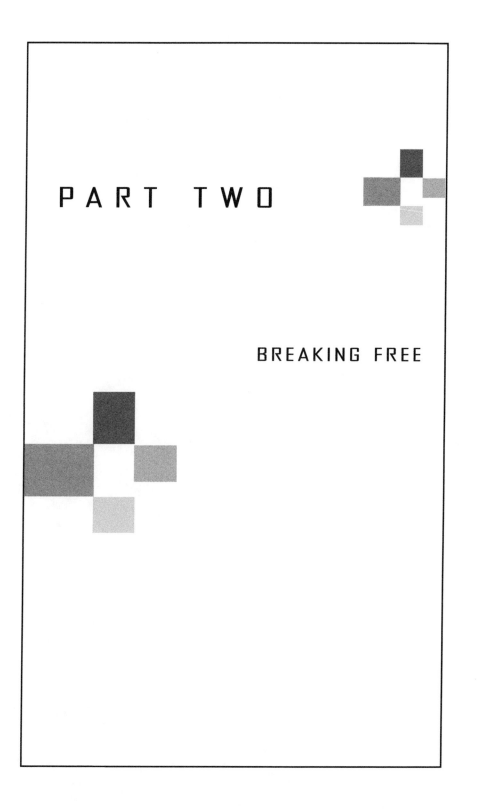

CHAPTER SIX

SHIFTING GEARS

How to Tame Anxiety and Banish Guilt

"Why do I always meet guys like Tim?" wondered Rebecca, the Clinger we met in Chapter 3. "I hate the fact that I'm in such a lopsided relationship, and I keep thinking that things will get better, but they never do. I'm so depressed."

"I love my husband, and of course I want to spend more time with him," said an anxious Kim, the Overdriver in Chapter 4. "But he's making me even more stressed and miserable by pressuring me to cut back on my work! I have a stack of papers a foot high on my desk. If I don't get to them, who will? Does he really expect me to let everyone in my office down?"

"If only I could convince Kerry how ridiculous it is for her to be upset that I can't make her son's birthday party," complained Patsy, the Serial Pleaser in Chapter 3. "I've always bent over backward to show her what a good friend I am. This time I have a really important pro-ject due, and I know I can't take two hours out for a five-year-old's party. Why can't she understand that—and why do I feel so bad about it?"

"Yes, I've always wanted to be a doctor," conceded Kathleen, Chapter 4's Career Martyr, "but I have a family to think about now. I wish I didn't feel so bored and useless, but sometimes plans don't al-ways work out. Sometimes you just have to put other people's needs ahead of your own. That's life. That's called being a grown-up."

That's also called being gridlocked.

I counsel people who are desperately unhappy with their lives but don't know what, or how, to change. If they do have a vision or goal for themselves, they're convinced that nothing they do could possibly make a difference. Stuck in the past, unable to function in—let alone enjoy—the present, they give up on the future. Few recognize the pow-erful, often interlocking feelings of anxiety and guilt that propel them to act in ways that render them helpless and trapped.

THE CRIPPLING EMOTIONS

By now you know that your early experiences powerfully affect your sense of identity—your ability to understand, trust, and feel good about who you are. In turn, your sense of identity shapes the way you, as an adult, relate to other people and the world at large, as well as the de-gree of ease or difficulty you have separating from them emotionally. By emotionally separating, I mean being able to recognize and respond to the needs of others in a healthy, appropriate manner and, at the same time, take care of your own needs. Unless you do, you'll inevitably be-come slowed down by, if not mired in, gridlock.

What makes this seemingly simple goal so elusive is that time and again your needs and the needs of others inevitably conflict. Let's say you want to push for a promotion at work, one that would generate more money and greater responsibility. But that step up the ladder for you may mean even less time with your husband, who really prefers having you home at night instead of tied to your office computer. If you go for the job challenge, you feel selfish, greedy. After all, you're not being a good enough wife. Or perhaps a close friend expects you to drop everything whenever she calls with her crisis of the moment, regardless of how late it is or how many times you've heard the same laments. When you beg out of the conversation, you feel unsupportive. After all, you're not being a good enough friend. Or perhaps you were raised to believe that a good daughter stays in touch regularly with her mother. You think a call every two days is sufficient. But whenever you phone home, she greets you with "Well, it's about time we heard from you." If your husband, friend, mother, or anyone else you care about sends the message that you are in some way not measuring up to expectations, your self-esteem takes a hit—sometimes a big one. Disappointing someone whose opinions matter makes many people feel anxious and guilty, like a naughty child who broke one of Mom's rules. Unconsciously, you think, "If I let them down, they'll get angry . . . they won't love me . . . I'll be alone. Then how will I manage?" Life becomes a constant jockeying of who gives and who gives up, who gets and who comes up empty. It is in the clash between wanting to please those we love or those whose approval we desire and needing to please ourselves that anxiety and guilt are born.

What's more, the tire tracks of anxiety and guilt lead directly to self-blame. Blasted by other people's disapproval or criticism, you may feel responsible for pleasing them and ashamed when you don't. If you're not clear about what you believe in or what you want to do, you may well accept their view of you as your own. Your overdeveloped sense of responsibility for people propels you deeper into gridlock, as you apologize for things that are not your fault and keep yourself stuck in situations that may be right for them but are all wrong for you. The internalized voice of negativity you heard when you were younger leads you to crash head-on into your own wall of self-blame. No wonder you grind your gears.

However, there is one point I cannot emphasize enough: As a child, you *were* totally helpless and dependent on someone else's (usually your parents') care and nurturing to feel loved, secure, and confident. You needed them to relieve your anxiety. Not anymore. Though it would be nice if the congratulations flowed, you no longer require their help to survive emotionally. When you're gridlocked, you may feel as if you can't function, but the truth is, you most definitely can.

Keep in mind that anxiety and guilt are not always hurtful or debilitating. A certain amount of anxiety is primal and instinctual—it keeps us from behaving in a foolhardy or dangerous way. A certain amount of guilt keeps us civilized and prevents us from doing things that might hurt ourselves or others. However, while everybody feels these negative emotions some of the time, you're reading this book because, too often, you have found yourself trapped in a maze of apologies, self-blame, pain, and paralysis. Too often you've short-circuited your journey and taken the road that felt safe and comfortable, albeit boring, unchallenging, and perhaps even dangerous to your emotional well-being. Too often you stayed stuck in a relationship, a job, a life situation that was wrong, not knowing it was possible to make it right and believing all the time that you couldn't handle whatever curveballs life threw your way. Instead of making necessary changes, you came to a grinding halt at the Stoplights—the fear of being alone, the fear of the unknown, the fear of intimacy, the fear of confrontation, and so on—that I flagged in the last three chapters. Your anxiety and guilt at the prospect of letting others down—perhaps engendering their anger and risking the loss of their love—prevented you from making your own emotional needs a priority.

It's time to put yourself in the driver's seat. The only way to successfully steer around anxiety and guilt—for the long term—is, first, to understand why their grip is so powerful. Then you can put safety measures in place that prevent you from succumbing to their pull.

Flip back to the Gridlock Questionnaire in Chapter 2. If you scored high, anxiety and guilt are still propelling you to enter new relationships or life situations weighed down by unfinished business. You're probably invalidating, denying, or minimizing your own needs, often feeling anxious or guilty when they emerge. You may feel that way, too, whenever you think about acting independently or doing something new. Acknowledging a difference of interest or opinion with someone you care about—and then doing it—can also trigger these crippling emotions. Even something seemingly unimportant—you want to go to the movies with your college roommate, but your spouse prefers to stay home and likes it when you're there, too; you're exhausted but agree to stay up night after night to watch Conan O'Brien; you agree to lend money to your sister, who just lost her job, when you'd been hoping to put those funds into refinishing the basement playroom—may cause you to put your interests and needs on the back burner as you expend time and psychic energy attending to others. In this chapter you'll learn how to take yourself seriously, as well as how to advocate on your own behalf.

However, breaking free of gridlock means more than simply making the decision to change, although that's a big one. It also means accepting the wrong turns as well as the potholes that you've run into so far. Your past may be riddled with unjust, failed, or hurtful events—or simply bad luck—but that doesn't sentence you to a lifetime of misery and deprivation. Nor does it give you the luxury of wallowing in your sorrow, forever regretting your lost opportunities—not if you want to change your life for the better. Realize that you can—indeed, must—take responsibility for your own life, because you can't change other people. You can only change how you relate to them and how they make you feel. Only then will you be able to recapture the joy of self-discovery and accomplishment.

In fact, no matter how long you've been stalled in neutral, no matter which rut you're stuck in—or even if you're stuck in more than one—you can begin right now to pump up your coping muscles. Remember, too, that you'll have to be willing to tolerate some anxiety and guilt in the short term if you want to achieve long-term gains. Like any muscle, your emotional coping muscles take time and repeated effort to develop. The objective isn't to rid yourself of all anxiety and guilt, but rather to be able to tolerate it while you find your way.

Consider the safety measures outlined here and in the next two chapters as your crash course in Driver's Ed. I've designed each skill to help you temper the anxiety and banish the guilt that program you for gridlock. By practicing these here-and-now techniques, you'll learn how to focus on and understand leftover childhood issues, as well as how to put new boundaries in place so that you can stay comfortably in your own lane and avoid head-on collisions with others. You'll learn how to soothe your anxiety—those restless, unsettled, jittery, inexplicably nervous feelings that keep you stuck and may even lead to self-destructive behaviors that compound gridlock, such as overeating, overspending, or abusing drugs or alcohol. You'll learn to use anxiety as a motivator so you feel freer to risk or start down a new path, while remaining calm and focused. And finally, you'll learn to quell your guilt so you can feel entitled and deserving when you do.

SAFETY MEASURE #1: CHART YOUR
EMOTIONAL ROAD MAP

When you're trying to break out of a rut, it helps to shine your high beams on what might have sent you careening off course in the first place. Consider: What events, situations, or experiences during your childhood might have contributed to your anxiety and guilt? The feelings of loss and abandonment that are the inevitable by-products of these circumstances can seriously affect your sense of security as well as your ability to trust yourself and others. What's more, if you never developed the means to alleviate these feelings, such experiences will exacerbate them.

Below, you'll find a list of circumstances that usually heighten anxiety and guilt. How many could be gridlocking you?

- Did your parents separate or divorce? If they divorced, did one parent pit you against the other, so you wound up feeling guilty if you wanted to spend time with them, or simply love them?
- Was a close family member very sick for a long period of time?
- Did your parent, or another close family member, abuse alcohol or drugs?
- Did one or both of your parents travel extensively on business?
- Did one or both of your parents work long hours?
- Was daily life punctuated by arguments? Did you feel worried, nervous, or lost in the conflict?
- Were your parents very critical of you? Did you often feel that you never measured up to the standards they set, that no matter what or how much you did, it was never enough?
- Did your parents overprotect you? Did they send the message that the world was a scary, dangerous place—and that you couldn't handle the challenge of change?
- Did your parents discourage your independent thinking or choices? Were they judgmental, controlling, critical, or unsupportive—beyond reason—of your choices in clothes, friends, activities, or interests?

- Were your parents often anxious and worried about you, your siblings, or their own lives in general?
- Did your family relocate to another town during a critical stage in your life?

Now try to remember the feelings you had, or still have, related to each specific event. How upsetting was each experience for you at the time? How did you and your family deal with it? Did you, or they, ignore it, never talk about it, or act as if it never happened? Did you, or they, stoically accept it and assume that there was nothing anyone could do? If you did, you may have a weak foundation for dealing with change now. By adopting the mantra "It's not so bad" or "Just forget about it," you and your family skirted some pivotal points. You may have learned to use denial and avoid feelings in order to carry on temporarily, without preparing yourself emotionally for the future. You'd be surprised how many people recite such past events or experiences to me as a matter of course, oblivious to the fact that the way they were handled years ago is affecting their current struggle.

For example, Elliott, the Clinger in Chapter 2, offhandedly mentioned that he'd always dreamed of being a foreign correspondent and wanted to attend Northwestern University because of its excellent journalism school. His father, however, had graduated from Yale and, come hell or high water, insisted that his only son do, too. Similarly, Annie, the Equalizer in Chapter 5, kept sharing her time and resources with her friend, despite the overwhelming evidence that her generosity wasn't reciprocated. In one conversation she casually told me about her younger sister, whom she'd always felt duty bound to make happy. Until I pointed it out, neither Elliott nor Annie had noticed a childhood pattern of feeling that they had never had a choice and had always deferred to a parent's or sibling's needs. By zeroing in on past events, you begin to develop the insight to be more self-aware. Once you do, you're on the road to discovering healthier ways to shore up your self-confidence and feel secure in your own right.

SAFETY MEASURE #2: READ THE ROAD SIGNS AND IDENTIFY YOUR PHANTOM FIGURES

As I said in Chapter 2, phantom figures are those people in your life now who cause you to act, and react, as you did with other significant people in your life long ago—most often, but not always, a parent or sibling. Unveiling your phantom figures, and determining whom they remind you of, is a powerful tool for smashing through gridlock, since it frees you from hurtful relationships and allows you to stop internalizing the negative voice of others as your own.

Nevertheless, tracing your phantom figure can be tricky. It's hard to link past experiences with current feelings, especially if you're no longer engaged in conflict with this person. People often believe that because they've distanced themselves from family members with whom they fought and are no longer actively engaged in disagreements with them, that these people couldn't possibly be affecting them now. They assume—wrongly—that their unmet emotional needs must be resolved. They don't realize that they are merely fighting the same old fight with someone else—always hoping that this time they'll be able to rewrite the script and finally get what they always wanted.

Focus on the love, work, or life relationship that is causing you the most difficulty right now. Then ask yourself this: With whom in your family of origin did you most often have difficulty? Whose acknowledgment did you crave? Whose approval meant the most to you? Does your current nemesis remind you of this person? That's your phantom figure. For example, Barbara, the woman in Chapter 1 who yearned to start a dance company, had a critical, rejecting mother whose approval she desperately wanted but never received. Once she homed in on that fact, she realized that she was continuing to experience the same conflict with her cousin Lisa. This recognition gave her the strength to stand up to Lisa and direct her energy toward more self-affirming steps, which I'll explain later in this chapter.

When looking for a phantom figure, pay attention to similarities in name, age, or appearance—particularly to siblings—that, astonishingly, people never see. Richard, the Bonder in Chapter 5, often clashed with his brother, Wayne, who was two years his senior. Now he's gridlocked in a Bonder relationship with his friend, who not only has the same name as his brother but is also two years older than he is. Unaware of the powerful pull from the past, Richard couldn't figure out why he was having so much difficulty putting limits on his friendship now. But once he reframed his current rut within the context of the difficult relationship he had with his brother, he was clearer and more confident about what he needed to do.

Once you determine who your phantom figure is, examine how that person makes you feel. Overpowered? Judged? Criticized? Selfish? Does he put you on the defensive? Do you often feel that you need to explain or justify your actions to him? Consider, too, if your negative experience with this person is an isolated event or if you often feel this way when you're with him, as well as whether you may be overreacting to what he is saying because you've been treated badly in the past and are very sensitive to any slights or perceived attacks. A tone, a word, a shrug of the shoulders may seem antagonistic because it reminds you of the way you used to be treated, even though it's not meant to be. Staying on top of this can help you pull back from the front lines of hostility and out of gridlock.

Why didn't you recognize this important connection before? After all, identifying a phantom figure seems so obvious that not to notice it seems akin to missing the entrance to a well-marked freeway. In truth, old feelings generated by old conflicts can be so engulfing, you simply can't see that what you're going through now is similar to where you've been.

After asking herself these questions, Patsy, the Serial Pleaser, realized that her friend Kerry was the phantom figure of her mother. Kerry made her feel guilty about not being a good enough friend in the same way her mother made her feel that she had never been a loving enough daughter. This helped Patsy begin to change her responses and behavior toward Kerry. She gave herself permission to do what she needed and wanted to do—that is, stay at work and complete her important presentation. She stopped apologizing over and over again to Kerry for not being there for her, because she finally had the conviction that her goal was highly valid. She also took an inventory of all the ways in which she had given to Kerry to show her how much she cared. (You'll learn to do this in Safety Measure #4.) In this way she affirmed her own beliefs of what constituted a "good" friend so she felt less anxious, less guilty, and more comfortable saying no to Kerry. You may not want to confront either, but you can still heal old wounds by readdressing them through a phantom figure—and this time taking responsibility for *your* emotional health, not *theirs*.

SAFETY MEASURE #3: ROLLING OUT OF A CHILDHOOD ROLE

Old roles present another huge hurdle that must be surmounted before you can get unstuck. The trouble is, they are often so much a part of how you are viewed by others that you've come to see yourself perfectly suited to them, too. Therein lies your next challenge.

With what label were you tagged? Perhaps you, like Kenny, the unemployed lawyer in Chapter 2 who was still living with his parents long after he'd graduated, were often treated like the family's black sheep. Or perhaps, like Denise in Chapter 4, you were the person everyone assumed would play a Mother Teresa–like role in all situations. No matter that the facts begged the question of the validity of that label, it stuck. And you came to believe it yourself.

You need to reject it now. To zoom in on your childhood label, consider your birth order (the first child is often expected to be a parent's helper or the high achiever who must do it all and do it well), your gender (some families place a high priority on being male, while others treat their daughters like princesses), the special talents or abilities you possess (the musician, the bright one, the athlete), as well as specific traits, positive or negative, you possess (the go-getter, the comedian, the lazy one).

Once you've highlighted your role, keep in mind that no matter how limiting or cumbersome it seems, you were getting something out of it, too. Kenny received financial support and a home to live in long past the time when most young adults support themselves. Wendy, the Braker in Chapter 5, never had to face possible rejection each time she made a phone call or submitted her résumé. Such psychological payoffs keep you stuck in your own personal comfort zone—but to break free of gridlock, you have to speed past them.

To do that, first list your own personal benefits from being stuck in that old role. Do you get a lot of attention? Do people feel sorry for you? Do they let you off the hook? If you're stuck here, ask a spouse or trusted friend what benefits he or she thinks you may be accruing from keeping yourself in a one-down position. Pay attention to the self-defeating messages you whisper to yourself that keep you coasting in your comfortable role. Are you blaming others for your situation, complaining but doing nothing? Once you rewrite that script and send yourself a positive message instead (see Safety Measure #4), you'll be better able to move toward a new vision of a more productive you.

For example, if you're gridlocked in work, think about the things in life that excite and interest you. What are your hobbies, your passions? Kenny realized that in law school, real-estate law was the one class he actually looked forward to and in which he did well. He decided to narrow his job search to a medium-size law firm that specialized in this area but would still give him room to grow. When he was finally offered an associate's spot, he anguished about whether he'd be able to hold his own and fit in with his colleagues. But, unlike his rejecting family, his co-workers actually gave him positive feedback. This time he listened to it, and instead of chastising himself for being inept, he began to acknowledge himself as competent and well informed, which in turn yielded even more rewards. When a colleague suggested he represent the firm by teaching a seminar class to first-year law students, Kenny squashed the old, self-defeating thoughts ("Me? I've never done that. . . . I couldn't possibly do that. . . .") and instead said, "I've never done that, but I'm game."

"You know what?" Kenny told me after his first class. "I was good at it. I really connected to the students." Kenny discovered that positive thinking is contagious. By confronting his anxiety and taking a risk, he was able to use his confidence as a motivating force. "I found myself speaking up more in meetings. I fully expected to be shot down, just like I'd always been at home. But it didn't happen. My colleagues took me seriously, and I started to take myself seriously, too. It felt great."

Envisioning himself as financially independent, he started to save a greater portion of his salary, which further boosted his self-esteem. Within a year he'd moved out of his parents' home and into his own apartment. He'd finally cast off his black-sheep role.

SAFETY MEASURE # 4: WATCH OUT
FOR POTHOLES

Potholes are all those critical, blaming messages and unrealistic expectations, overt or covert, that can easily throw you off the road. To avoid them, you have to know where they are and develop a protective strategy to steer around them.

If you feel anxious or guilty (or, of course, angry, which I'll get to in Chapter 7) whenever you're with someone, that's often a red flag that you are depending too heavily on that person's approval and may be gridlocked by anxiety and guilt. When you're gridlocked, you automatically brush aside, rationalize, minimize, or deny your responses. Pay attention to them now. Keep a "feeling meter" of all the emotions that swirl inside you each day, especially in regard to the people or situations in which you feel most stuck. Do you feel inadequate? Stupid? Ignored? Worthless? Anxious? Greedy? Thoughtless? Inconsiderate? Selfish?

Now think about how the expectations and goals you have for yourself—your personal "shoulds" list—clash with those that other people have for you.

Let's say you're gridlocked in a hurtful relationship, as Andrea, the Bonder, was with Jody, the friend she met in Lamaze class. On a sheet of paper, list all the things your friend accuses you of doing or not doing—in other words, what *she* thinks you should be doing. Next to that, jot down how her belief makes you feel. Andrea wrote:

- Jody believes I shouldn't go back to work. (Andrea's translation: "My judgment about what's important in life is all screwed up.")
- She thinks I should spend more time with my daughter (Andrea's translation: "I'm a terrible mother.")
- She says I'm not there for her anymore. (Andrea's translation: "I'm not a good friend.")

Now list all the qualities *you* believe are hallmarks of a good friend. Your list might look like this one:

A good friend is:

supportive

understanding

available to listen and help

To avoid "should" collisions, you must develop a working definition tailored to what you do give as well as what you want to give. That definition must have some clear, built-in limits. If you're going to get unstuck, you can no longer operate under the rule of pleasing everyone all the time. By recognizing your needs and acknowledging how you see things differently from other people, you develop self-confidence and strengthen your individuality. Flesh out your list with specifics. If you wrote that a friend should be available to listen, what exactly does that mean to you? All the time? Whenever a friend calls, no matter how late? If you think it means being supportive, does that mean you must always agree with your friend, or can you ever disagree?

Contrast your expectations with those of the person with whom you're gridlocked. How relevant, reasonable and realistic are they? Is she making some valid points? Or is she expecting you to sacrifice too much? The gap between your "should" list and the "should" list of others generates your anxiety and guilt.

By charting your expectations in this way, you'll begin to feel good about yourself, because you will be determining what is right for you independent of the opinions of others. It is this emotional separation that enables you to see more clearly the lane in which *you* want to travel—a vital boundary for emotional health.

NOTE: Be aware of key phrases or comments that derail many people and cause "should" collisions. These are the flashing yellow lights that warn of "should" collisions ahead:

- "If you loved me, then you would . . ."
- "You're supposed to . . ."
- "It's about time."
- "You don't care about me."
- "It's always what you want."
- "Yes . . . but." (Countering the positive with a negative, as in "Yes, you called, but not until two days after my crisis."

SAFETY MEASURE #5: CHANGE YOUR CD (YOUR INNER CRITICAL DIALOGUE)

Now that you've navigated around potholes and skirted "should" collisions, it's time to change the gridlocking CD you've been playing inside your head. You do this by transforming self-defeating messages into self-affirming ones. Changing your inner critical dialogue—which reflects the way you feel about yourself and your possibilities for the future—is essential for moving forward. Athletes have known this for years. Watch a tennis player pace the baseline before a match and you'll catch him muttering words of encouragement to himself. Ditto for speed skaters or marathon runners. In fact, numerous studies have shown that when people talk positively to themselves as they work, their words help them focus their concentration, defuse tense situations, and boost self-confidence.

Self-approval stems from self-acceptance and the clear acknowledgment of what you can do and where you can go, no matter where you've been before. To shift from a gridlocking "I can't/I'm not" stance to a self-affirming "I can/I will" stance, focus on the way you're feeling right now. Below are a few tip-offs that your CD is a critical and self-defeating one. How many crop up on a regular basis?

If only...

What if...

I should have...

Everyone else... Or: All the people who started college with me...

Critical dialogue is also suffused with general ways of thinking and observing that gridlock people time and again. The ones I see most often are:

HORRIBILIZING: Thinking only the worst; blowing things completely out of proportion. "Gee, I forgot to call Steve back. He's going to be so angry, and he'll blame me, and when he tells everyone else, then the whole family will be upset."

ALL-OR-NOTHING THINKING: Moves you into an either/or mode, with no room for flexibility, strategizing, or compromising. "I didn't get that promotion; I'm obviously in the wrong field." "Either we get married or the relationship is over."

GLOBALIZING: General statements, no specifics. Perhaps you tell yourself, "I'm just lazy." "He's just selfish." Or: "I never . . ." or "I always . . ."

PERFECTIONISM: No errors, all losses. You focus only on what you didn't do or what failed to work, rather than on what you have accomplished. "I killed myself on that report, but there was a small mistake in the chart on page fifty-six. No one else will notice, but I can't believe I was so careless."

BACK-TO-THE-FUTURE THINKING: Assumptions and predictions based only on the past. "It's never worked before. I've never been able to . . ." which leads to "I never will be able to . . ."

To change the critical dialogue that holds you back, keep a small notebook handy and write down every negative thought that races through your head whenever it does—the things you're afraid of or worried about, where you feel you're stuck, or why you don't think you can move ahead. (Refer back to Safety Measure #2 or #4 if you need to.) Structure your list in two columns, one headed "Why I Don't Want to Do This" (that is, all the minuses) and one headed "Why I Want to Do This" (all the pluses). Look at all the critical words or phrases in your minus list that are holding you back, and focus on the positives that you stand to gain if you do move ahead. Seeing on paper the thoughts that routinely gridlock you is an excellent way to remind yourself that you may be your own worst enemy. Keep this piece of paper in your wallet and refer to it from time to time.

The next step in changing the CD is learning to apologize to yourself. Forgiving yourself instead of forgiving everyone else cuts through self-blame and paves the road to self-acceptance. Recognizing your limitations or vulnerabilities helps you zone in on where and how you want to improve. And when you're less defensive, you're better prepared to handle other people's gridlocking behavior. The four steps in a Self-Apology include:

- Acknowledge what you did or didn't do that has made you feel anxious, guilty, and gridlocked.
- Consider what made you do it, or what might have prevented you from behaving the way you wanted to.
- Clarify what you learned.
- Recognize how you'll do things differently in the future.

Let's say you've been stewing about asking your boss for a long-overdue raise, but every time you had an opportunity to promote yourself, you lost your nerve. Use the Self-Apology to stop clubbing yourself for the past, and instead focus on what you will say to counter any negative self-talk right now. Running the positive dialogue in your head will help you organize your thoughts and dispel anxiety. You might say, "I am a dependable hardworking employee, with a good track record that I've outlined in this memo. I'm really committed to this firm, and I believe I can help it grow. I'd like to be given the opportunity."

SAFETY MEASURE #6: SKID CONTROL

When you feel that you're moving into an emotional danger zone, you need to shift to your protective gears so you can stay in control. This exercise is not designed to change other people's minds or get them to agree with you. They may always have different opinions, perceptions, or values. The goal here is to help you stay calm and confident of your own choices and steadfast in the face of oncoming traffic so you can respond to "should" collisions with empathy and grace. Keep the following points in your emotional glove compartment. They will help you disengage from those who are gridlocking you, so you can accept who they are, and at the same time separate emotionally from them.

First, think about your knee-jerk reactions in the face of the judgmental or deprecating comments of others. Few of us are immune to such barbs, but we all react in typical ways. Some withdraw into silence. Others lash out angrily, or launch a tit-for-tat attack ("Well, you do the same thing, so what's the difference?") Still others resort to countering ("Well, I did that because you did this"). Once you recognize the style you've been using to defend yourself, you can begin to change. From now on, try:

USING HUMOR: If someone consistently hits you with a "should" or a negative comment, turn it into a game. You probably know precisely when your mother, or your husband, is going to be critical or demeaning. Play detective and try to anticipate this behavior. Once you can spot a negative comment before it's lobbed your way, you'll be able to finesse it with an appropriate response. When you do, you'll no longer be gridlocked by your old fantasy that someday, somehow, this person will treat you any differently. Instead, you'll come to see and accept people for who they really are.

To wit: If you know your mother is going to criticize the fact that you still haven't found a job, the next time you speak to her, see how long it takes her to let go with her typical zinger and chuckle to yourself if you guessed right. Prepare your own answer to her comment that will let her know you know precisely what she's doing. One woman in just this predicament said, "You're absolutely right, I still haven't found a job—it's good you noticed!" She wasn't hostile or nasty. She was cool but sharp. And her point hit home.

ACKNOWLEDGING THEIR COMMENTS OR FEELINGS: Learn to empathize by putting yourself in the other person's shoes. Imagine if the situation were reversed, and *you* were the one demanding more time or attention. How would you feel? Andrea, the Bonder in Chapter 5, told her friend Jody, "I know it feels to you like I won't be there for you if I go back to work part-time, but that's not the case." Empathizing doesn't mean you have to make people feel better by fixing their problems. It simply means you acknowledge their anger or disappointment.

For example, Donna, the Staller in Chapter 3, whose husband, Brad, was furious that she wanted to take a writing course in the evening, in time learned to say, "Brad, I should have told you the truth about where I was going from the beginning. I know you're upset because you want me to spend time with you. I'd like to do that, but it's also important that I do the things I value as well. Writing is one of them." By asserting her own feelings, Donna curbed her anxiety about attending class and assuaged her guilt by showing concern for Brad's feelings. Sure, he's not thrilled with her choice. But because of her caring, honest manner, rather than her old distant, deceitful behavior, he's not taking it so personally and no longer feels rejected.

PUTTING YOUR FEELINGS ON THE TABLE: Use the "When you . . . then I feel . . ." formula. For instance: "When you grill me about my job hunt, then I feel like I'm letting you down. I'm looking as hard as I can, and when I find something, I'll let you know." The key is to address the behavior only in terms of how it affects you. Otherwise, it will sound as if you're being critical, and the person will be defensive instead of responsive.

DEFLECTING IT: Go with the flow. You can say, "I hear what you're saying, but I think this is a good move for me." Or "You're right. I'm finally calling" (no excuses, explanations, end of discussion—move on to something else).

CONSIDERING IT: Be open-minded. You can afford to make room for what someone wants to say as long as you remember that you don't need his or her approval to do what you want to do. "I'll certainly think about what you said" or "Thank you for your concern" is good enough. Nor do you have to reveal your plans or ideas, just because someone asked. Learn to *edit the information* you give others. Many people, like Annie, are gridlocked because they believe that they're being selfish or deceptive if they don't tell everything all the time. Annie, for instance, realized that her phantom figure—Michelle—was a substitute for her younger sister. Annie was convinced that she had to share everything with her little sister, and she frequently compromised her own interests to make sure her sister was happy and everything was "fair." As a result, she is still giving away her resources and advice. In time she recognized that she was entitled to be selective about what she divulged to her friend. Comments such as "Gee, I'd rather not talk about that" or "You know, I did buy this at Macy's, but I'd prefer if you didn't get the same thing" now come to her lips more easily.

Skid control also means *never picking up a hitchhiker.* Serial Pleasers, Equalizers, Clingers, Stallers, Career Martyrs, and Care Seekers in particular need to be wary of this. They, more than others, fall into the I-feel-so-sorry-for-him-and-I-need-to-make-it-better trap. When you pick up a hitchhiker, you may be forced to go out of your way and into dangerous territory. Instead, hold the other person accountable for getting himself wherever he needs to go, as well as for producing what he promised to do for you.

Finally, Skid Control includes knowing when and how to *use the shoulder.* If you're really dead-ended, you must stop shouldering all the responsibilities for the problem and instead pull over and get off the road—in other words, realize that a relationship or situation may be damaged beyond repair. It's very common for gridlocked people to take such failure personally. Keep in mind that your need for attachment is keeping you gridlocked, pushing you to tolerate a bad relationship or a bad job on the pretext that nothing else is available or possible. Although I've found that such an assumption is usually not the case, in Chapters 7 and 8 you'll learn how to back up or pull out if it is.

SAFETY MEASURE #7: START YOUR ENGINE

Now you're prepared to map out where you want to go. Be sure to set goals that are realistic and attainable—nothing succeeds like success. To ensure that, divide large, general goals into specific, mini ones. Imagining that you're going to write the next bestseller is too daunting to be doable, more likely to be put off than accomplished. But vowing to write in a journal—a poem, a paragraph, a short story—is doable. Plan the amount of time you think it will take to accomplish each step toward your goal as well as when you're going to begin and when you'll take pit stops, or breaks, along the way. By carefully structuring your work time, you avoid overwhelming yourself with anxiety that you can't do the task and instead remain calm and tolerant of changes as you move closer toward your goal. An added benefit: You'll experience the exhilaration of doing, and actually completing, something long postponed. The trick is to focus on the fun, not the fear.

For example, if you're a Braker gridlocked about making a job change, plan to get your résumé written, printed, and mailed in, say, one month, not one week. First, structure your week so you can block out time to write it. What are your other commitments? Tune in to your habits, tailoring your schedule to the most productive times of your day. Are you a morning or a late-night person? Do you concentrate better on the weekend? Where do you do your best work—at a desk or a table or lying on the bed listening to music? When you are sensitive to your physical and emotional needs, you can recharge your battery and carry on. Once you've begun, focus on that task and only that task, resisting the temptation to pick up the phone or flip on the TV, and praise yourself when you complete it! If you fail to accomplish what you set out to do one day, don't berate yourself. Reevaluate instead. When Wendy, the Braker in Chapter 4, first sat down to write her résumé, she pushed herself to work for three hours and then scheduled a thirty-minute snack and TV-watching break. It didn't work: Her breaks were stretching to an hour or more, and she was irritable and frustrated by day's end. Instead of beating herself up and then giving up, she used the Self-Apology and decided to work for no more than one hour, then break for fifteen minutes. This pace suited her better, and she pulled her résumé and portfolio together in record time.

SAFETY MEASURE #8: DOWNSHIFTING

Another way to transform anxiety and guilt into excitement is to find ways to calm down so you aren't afraid to keep trying. Downshifting involves doing whatever you need to do to feel better, safer, and capable of carrying on—and it's a very personal choice. Instead of steering away from negative feelings (your worn-out tools of minimizing, denying, or rationalizing them), use your feelings as arrows to your emotional needs and figure out what small steps you can take to quell anxiety as you move toward your goal. *Learn to take care of yourself by caring for yourself.* Remember Elliott, the Clinger who had broken his engagement several times but still couldn't end the relationship? Elliott was convinced he couldn't manage without a woman in his life. To tackle his separation anxiety, he made a few concrete changes that he hadn't attempted before, because either his fiancée wasn't interested or, he claimed, he didn't have time: He enrolled in a gym and learned to play racquetball. He consulted a nutritionist and began to take better care of his health. From time to time throughout the day, he reminded himself of the self-affirming messages he'd jotted down to ease his nervousness. He also *learned to distract himself,* another useful technique for easing anxiety. Whenever he was doing something new or alone, such as going out to dinner or to a movie, as soon as he started to feel nervous, he would get up, walk outside, or go to the bathroom. This simple distraction took his mind off the anxiety until it passed.

Downshifting also means that if anxiety or guilt is escalating too fast for your emotional safety, you may need to *take your foot off the gas.* Many people, especially those who are just realizing that they're stuck, have a sense of urgency to do something immediately to break free of gridlock. They think change must happen right away. In truth, change is a process—you were stuck for a long time, and it will take time to get unstuck.

For this to happen, you must develop patience so you can manage the frustration of a new learning experience. Setbacks and mistakes are inevitable, and you may make a bad choice. That's why they put erasers on pencils. *Ask yourself, How were mistakes handled in your family?* Were they deemed irrevocable? Did a parent or sibling hold them against you and attack you with them time and again? Did you believe you would never recover from a mistake, no matter how small it was? To further promote your own emotional separation, adopt a new, self-accepting style. Invoke your learner's permit: Instead of using a mistake to condemn yourself, allow for do-overs and use the experience to foster emotional and intellectual awareness.

SAFETY MEASURE #9: PREPARE FOR DEPARTURE

Once you make a change—however slight—in a relationship or situation in which you've been gridlocked, you'll move through an emotional separation much like the toddler or preschooler who must say good-bye to his parents at the nursery-school door. As I said in the very first chapter of this book, change of any kind involves loss, so be prepared for a certain amount of anxiety, awkwardness, sadness, or other discomfort as a result. Stress may manifest itself psychologically or physically, so be sensitive to yourself and allow others to give to you and be there for you if you need support. Remind yourself that while these feelings may border on the painful, they are the temporary growing pains that accompany the separation process. In fact, by being labeled as such, they provide the proof that you're becoming more independent.

To ease the way, begin to stock your emotional reserves by seeking out encouragement from others. Don't be stoic and try to go it alone. This is the time to let others be there for you. Call someone you can trust—your mother, a friend, a sibling. Don't call someone who tends to respond in an I-told-you-so manner. And remind yourself that growing pains are necessary and normal, so take it slowly if you have to. Kathleen, the Career Martyr who had forsaken a lifelong dream to be a doctor to raise her children, felt overwhelming guilt that she had abandoned her family by applying and enrolling in medical school. She also felt sad, as she shifted from being a full-time mother to a student. But she balanced those negative feelings by allowing her new colleagues and friends to validate her work and participation. This led to feelings of acceptance and appreciation for her new self—the one who was less irritable and more tolerant and happier. "I knew I had fewer hours to spend with my kids, but I really made the most of them," she told me. "It became much more quality time, because I paid attention to them more." To her delight and surprise, they were not angry with her, as she had feared, but rather excited and acknowledging of her change.

SAFETY MEASURE #10: JUST GET MOVING

Trust me on this one: It's more important to be moving ahead—doing something, anything, to change a gridlocking situation—than it is to be 100-percent certain about the direction you're moving in. Too many people stay stuck because they can't precisely envision where they want to go or specifically what they want to do. They often predicate making a change on first having to do something else—lose ten pounds, move to a new apartment, get a boyfriend. They put their lives on hold because they're waiting for opportunity to knock. Or they write off their own talents and abilities as "pure luck," not understanding that we create our own luck by harnessing our energies, taking chances, and making opportunities happen. Those in gridlock procrastinate, deem themselves unlucky, or wallow in wishful thinking, dreaming that the perfect job, the perfect man, the perfect opportunity for breaking free will mysteriously appear.

Jennifer, an editorial assistant at a magazine and a victim of the Impostor Syndrome I described in Chapter 4, seduced herself into waiting for opportunity to knock. She didn't feel as qualified as her co-workers, though she certainly was, and she avoided taking any initiative. For years she made excuses for herself: "I can't look for a new job because I need to have more experience" . . . "This place is like a family to me. How can I give up what I have?" . . . "What if I can't handle a new job? That would prove that my career choice was wrong all along." Jennifer waited for someone to call and ask her to take a new, more responsible position. She waited seventeen years.

You don't need to wait for the highway to clear before getting on either. By now you've developed driving skills to stay safe even in traffic. Take the better route: Use your fears to motivate you. Whether it's making that first call to a friend who has placed one too many demands on you or contacting the personnel department about a job change, no one is going to read your mind. *Change the CD* so you feel more capable and in control. Then check your list of attainable goals (Safety Measure #7) and make one small change at a time. Ask questions, network, do research. As you meet new people or encounter different situations, your experiences will generate new ideas for even more alternate routes. Confidence comes with the doing, propelling you out of gridlock.

Jennifer finally structured her goal of finding a more creative position one task at a time. She wrote down the steps she needed to take, such as meeting colleagues at other magazines for lunch, accepting invitations to press conferences and PR luncheons she'd previously discarded so she could research what other publications were like and hear about possible personnel changes. After writing her résumé and cover letter, she mailed them to five magazines where she wanted to work and followed up each letter a week later with a phone call. "Five phone calls I could handle," she said. "And I lined up three interviews." Jennifer was on her way.

In the next chapter I'll discuss how you can manage the gridlocking emotion of anger. Anger, together with anxiety and guilt, not only keeps you stuck, it destroys any positive work you may have already accomplished in moving forward.

CHAPTER SEVEN

PUT THE BRAKES

ON ANGER

How to Move Back Without Pulling Out

There's nothing wrong with getting angry. But *staying* angry is one of the main reasons you're gridlocked. Let me explain.

Anger has gotten a bad rap. We tend to think all anger is negative, something we have to get rid of. In truth, anger—recognized and effectively channeled—can be a potent, mobilizing tool for smashing gridlock and summoning the courage for real change. Anger can invigorate a stalled life and actually help you solve the problems that sparked your ire in the first place. But you need to learn how to transform it. Anger is energy that can be directed to either constructive or destructive ends. Like gasoline in the tank of a car, anger contained is fuel that can carry you toward your goal. Spilled on the ground, it's an explosion waiting to happen.

Anger is a signal that something, somewhere in your life is wrong.

It cues you in to the fact that one of your fundamental needs—to be valued, respected, appreciated, acknowledged, loved, and understood—is not being met. You may not realize that when these needs are thwarted, you don't just feel mad and agitated; you may also feel sad, worthless, and rejected. What's more, those feelings can further trigger a range of hot emotions, from frustration and indignation to explosive rage.

The trouble is, anger is also a shield, and a false one at that, temporarily masking those painful but necessary feelings. To break out of gridlock, you need to face them—now.

People mistakenly assume that the only way to handle a situation or relationship that angers them is to make a radical change. Paradoxically, this actually perpetuates gridlock by boxing you into a stay-or-leave corner. In fact, there may actually be a number of small steps you can take, or options you can examine, before you take the big step of pulling away entirely from a situation that has you gridlocked.

In this chapter you'll learn how to negotiate for that middle ground. You'll find out how to use your energy to stay in your relationship or situation while you reshape it and see if it's possible to make it better. Using your anger to problem-solve effectively allows you to preserve your self-esteem, boost your self-respect, and take charge of your life. You'll learn to focus on the internal (what you're feeling and what changes you can make) rather than on the external (what's being done to you, what's happening to you, what you can't do anything about). Instead of blaming others for your distress or vainly attempting to convince them to change—which will only make you feel even more helpless, dependent, and stuck—you'll be able to identify your needs and the subsequent feelings that get evoked when they're not met.

Many people resent the fact that they may have to do something to change a situation that seems unfair. "Why should I change?" they complain. "It's his fault." Or I hear "She's the problem, not me. It's not fair." My answer to them is, It may not be fair, but it is necessary. If you don't do something, nothing will happen. Effectively using your anger means taking responsibility for what is upsetting you and then taking the steps you need to take to make you happier. As long as you keep on waiting for someone else to do the changing, you'll stay gridlocked.

Once you give yourself permission to be angry, you will no longer be so overwhelmed by the feeling. Most significantly, when you are able to recognize, accept, and manage your own anger, you will be less frightened of other people's anger. You'll feel less intimidated and therefore freer to assert your position, clear the road of obstacles, and make significant changes in your life.

BURIED RAGE

We tend to think that anger is all temper tantrums, slammed doors, and thrown plates. But anger can also simmer and smolder on a low flame for years, cloaked behind a range of emotional and physical symptoms and wreaking havoc with your personal or work life. In fact, anger may be buried so deeply, or camouflaged so successfully, that you may be aware of it for a millisecond. Its destructive impact, however, is well documented.

Anger accumulates slowly as small stresses pile up. When it does, your heart races and your blood pressure soars, increasing the risk of heart attack. Venting your anger can be as pernicious as stuffing it inside. When you yell or shout "You idiot!" at your insensitive boyfriend (or the computer that just crashed), you rev your internal motor, pump up your blood pressure, and heighten the psychological and physical havoc. Either way, you're doing nothing to better your own situation, but you are paving the way for anger to render you depressed and more vulnerable to a host of stress-related illnesses and symptoms: headaches, sleep difficulties, sexual problems, and eating disorders, to name a few. Think of anger as a balloon filled with air. You can squeeze the air out of one end, but it fills up elsewhere.

Women especially don't get much practice with anger. They're taught that it's unladylike, socially taboo. Better to suppress it than express it. Better to sacrifice intimacy than risk rage. "No, of course I'm not angry," you say with the too-bright smile, though your stomach is roiling like an ocean in a hurricane. After all, no one will like you, let alone love you, if you're angry. They'll call you hostile, bitchy, hysterical, shrewish, demanding. They'll assume you have your period. "I'm not mad," you insist to your husband, mother, friend, or sister through gritted teeth, though you hate being treated like a doormat and feel as if you've been punched in the stomach. Instead of discussing an issue that has you gridlocked, you withdraw into a perpetually peeved mode, complaining, nagging, and cranky. "I'm not angry; I understand," though a plum project that should have been yours was just awarded to a less deserving colleague.

What's more, because we're socialized to believe that being angry is bad, many people don't give their angry feelings the legitimacy that they deserve. Unable to discriminate between anger that's misplaced and anger that's appropriate, they second-guess themselves and wonder, "Should I really be this upset? Maybe he's right . . . maybe I am making a mountain out of a molehill." Because they don't believe they have a right to be angry, because they aren't equipped to fend for themselves and set limits, they are literally at a loss for words. They feel guilty, back off, and begin to store their anger inside. In time that anger reaches a kindling point. One small affront ratchets up their level of anger and unleashes a flood of self-righteous wrath as all semblance of rational thought dissolves.

However, when this happens, whatever point they were trying to make will become obliterated by their own road rage, and they are easily dismissed by the person with whom they're gridlocked. "You're like a crazy person," snapped Brad, the husband of Donna, the Staller in Chapter 3, as he laughingly disparaged her desire to attend a writing seminar. "I can't talk to you when you're this out of control." Her angry reactions provided a smoke screen he could hide behind to avoid dealing with the issues she was trying to raise. As long as she continued to do that, she let him off the hook.

While Donna exploded in fury, others who don't believe they have a right to be angry fall into a defensive mode, overexplaining their needs and feelings. As you'll see in the next chapter, they are easily thrown into a tailspin whenever someone counters them. They feel as helpless and vulnerable as they did when they were young. Paradoxically, in the heat of anger they may actually feel a false sense of power, one that propels them to act irrationally and precipitously— such as quitting a job before they have found a new one. Or by saying, "This relationship is over." The trouble is, they are unable to sustain their anger over a period of time in order to use it effectively to set limits against intolerable behavior. Unless they truly feel entitled to their feelings and believe in their own right to be angry, they quickly capitulate, overwhelmed with guilt and fear, and often apologize for their outburst and end up feeling even more dependent, helpless, and stuck.

Still others are gridlocked because they don't want to relinquish their anger. Resentful and bitter at the way they've been treated, they store up small hurts for a long time, and may even refuse an apology ("It's too little, too late") and use it to further justify their indignation. Holding tightly to a grudge feels empowering and gives them license to maintain their fury and punish whoever wronged them. The apology validates that they were indeed mistreated and provides a green light for them to stay that way. Jackie, the Staller in Chapter 3 who stayed stuck for years in an unhappy marriage, held a grudge for so long that it prevented her from effectively tapping her anger and using it to at least try to redesign her marriage to Jeff. Instead of speaking up and looking for opportunities for change, she just stayed angry and never even got near enough to problem solving to see if her marriage could have been saved.

THE MANY FACES OF ANGER

Most people have so little experience dealing appropriately with anger that they often don't recognize it at all. They don't realize that annoyance, irritation, and frustration are at one end of the same emotional continuum as out-of-control fury and explosiveness. It took a long time before Eric, the System Saboteur in Chapter 4, conceded that his chronic lateness to office meetings was linked to his jealousy and resentment of his new colleague. Annie, the Equalizer in Chapter 5, didn't realize how much she really resented her friend Bonnie, although she kept wishing that she would move away or somehow just disappear from her life. Similarly, Stephanie, the Bouncer in Chapter 3, thought she was in love with another man. She didn't realize that her lack of sexual interest for her husband was rooted in her anger at him for controlling nearly every aspect of her life. In fact, many people are mystified by their diminished sexual desire and never make the connection between their angry feelings for their spouse and their loss of interest in sex. But the truth is, if you're heated up in anger, it's hard to feel the heat of passion in bed.

Indeed, we show our rage in myriad ways, some internalized, others externalized. Below, I've charted the most common clues to buried anger. Consider whether any reflect the way you act or what you say to others:

INTERNALIZERS. *If you are a Clinger, Staller, Office Personalizer, System Saboteur, Career Martyr, Serial Pleaser, Bonder, Equalizer, or Care Seeker, you're most likely to reveal anger by:*

Swallowing or hiding your feelings; storing up old hurts.

Withdrawing in silence or giving someone the cold shoulder.

Shooting lethal looks of disapproval.

Saying you'll do something but "forgetting" to do it.

Exhibiting provocative, running-red-light behavior: Agreeing to do something, then breaking your agreement without first discussing why or without negotiating another option.

Blaming yourself.

Doing a tit-for-tat: "Well, he did it, so I can, too."

Concocting elaborate methods of revenge; fantasizing.

Self-sabotaging, self-destructive behaviors: Overeating; taking drugs; using alcohol; spending money excessively; "forgetting" to do something; or slipping into a "why bother?" stance. As Jackie, the Staller, told me, "Why should I even bother talking to Jeff? It's a waste of time."

Lying or withholding information.

Indirectly coercing or manipulating others ("I'm too busy to take care of that broken answering machine. If you want it fixed so badly, you'll have to take it to the shop yourself.")

EXTERNALIZERS. *If you're a Distancer, Bouncer, Overdriver, Office Personalizer, or System Saboteur, you're most likely to show anger by:*

Exploding.

Making cutting, hostile, sarcastic remarks; name-calling, "teasing" or poking fun at someone's vulnerabilities, as in: "You don't really need that piece of cake, do you? Hey, why are you getting so upset? I'm only kidding!"

Creating allies and colluding with others.

Saying you'll do something but deliberately not doing it.

Retaliating by using sex as a weapon; spending money; staying out late.

Rebelling or responding with self-righteous indignation.

Issuing hollow threats: "If you don't stop, that's it. I want a divorce!"

Overreacting to unimportant or trivial events; purposely instigating or prolonging a fight.

Chronically complaining or whining about what you don't like or didn't want.

Keep in mind that the way you handle and respond to anger, as well as the issues that make you angry, are in large part determined by what you saw modeled by your parents or other family members when you were younger. If you come from a long line of shouters, you may feel it's perfectly natural and acceptable to yell and scream when you're upset. On the other hand, if you felt intimidated and threatened by a parent's fury, you may now be so frightened of your own or someone else's wrath that you avoid it at all costs, even if that means squashing your true feelings or caving in to unreasonable demands. Also, if your parents routinely upbraided you or spoke in an abusive, dismissive, rude manner, you may be easily upset by such a tone now, or even find yourself speaking this way to others.

Rebecca, the Clinger in Chapter 3, was anger-phobic. Whenever she tried to express vexation as a child, her older brother made her feel so spoiled and selfish that her guilt immediately rose up and blocked her anger. As a result, she continued to tolerate inappropriate behavior, and caved in to her brother in much the same way she yields to her boyfriend Tim now.

The way you were raised may have also contributed to a number of anger myths I hear about often. As long as you still believe them, you'll perpetuate your anger style and stay stuck.

Anger and rage don't belong in a healthy relationship.

If I get angry, I will lose all control.

If people are angry with me, it's my fault.

I should feel guilty if I get angry.

I'm selfish if I get angry.

I'm bad if I upset someone.

If I get upset, I'll be abandoned.

Fighting makes a relationship seem dramatic and exciting.

Fighting makes us closer, so it's worth it.

Each of these statements is false—yet those who believe them are dismissing a valuable gridlock-smashing tool. As you'll see, anger constructively channeled can help you step back from a provocative situation and figure out how to move on.

RX FOR ANGER

But first you need to decode the deeper message your anger is trying to send you. Once you do, you can better determine if your anger is valid or if you're overreacting and being too sensitive. Don't forget that the intensity of your anger is not always an accurate measurement. As I've pointed out, at times you may be particularly sensitive to things that are said or done because of your past history and hurts. The effects of anger are cumulative, and as even minor annoyances or irritations pile up, the level of your anger increases and your engine may quickly flood or overheat. To wit: You may become infuriated when your husband forgets to pick up the dry cleaning, not understanding that what is really upsetting you is the fact that for the past few months he's rarely paid attention to anything you said. On the other hand, his forgetfulness may simply be due to the fact that he's been preoccupied with problems at work or was running late that day to an important meeting and didn't have time. Or he might simply have forgotten, with no other ulterior motive. Your job is to separate the behaviors that are frustrating but tolerable from those that are hurtful and must be changed.

To make sure your anger doesn't lead you in the wrong direction, stop and check your rearview mirror as well as the route ahead. Give yourself time to think about what may be sparking your anger in the first place. Figure out which behaviors are truly about you and which may merely be due to another person's carelessness, fatigue, miscommunication, or other concerns at the moment. To track your personal triggers, keep an "anger journal" and jot down each time you feel or respond with anger. What circumstances or actions prompted you to do this? Was your response effective, or did it backfire? Can you detect any patterns?

Ask yourself: Underneath your anger, do you feel sad, mad, vexed, hurt, unloved, worthless, inadequate, or rejected . . .

. . . when someone uses certain words or phrases in addressing you?

. . . when you have to repeat yourself several times?

. . . when someone doesn't follow through on a promise?

. . . when someone treats you in a condescending way?

. . . when it seems as if someone else is getting special treatment and you're not?

. . . when someone forgets your birthday or some important moment or accomplishment in your life?

. . . when someone appears to be telling you what to do?

. . . when someone questions your judgment or doubts your abilities or intelligence?

Consider, too, whether a person makes you feel this way all the time or only once in a while. Is this display of thoughtlessness common, or is this particular incident unusual? Does he or she ever give, or do, for you? This will help you put the experience in context and take things less personally. If you realize that at times the person is there for you, hold on to that awareness and use it to soften your anger so you can respond with empathy to what prompted this behavior. Even if it does happen frequently, you can still bring some objectivity to bear by recognizing that it may simply be that person's own failing—he's never on time to anything; she always speaks loudly when she gets excited—and not a comment on his or her respect, concern, or love for you.

Also evaluate whether you display the same hundred pounds of anger in every circumstance, regardless of the situation. Start to discriminate between those that are really important, and reflect problems that must be addressed, and those that require more patience and tolerance on your part. To break free of gridlocking anger, it's essential that you learn to temper your reactions and put them in perspective, instead of storing them up and sliding into a slow burn until you explode in fury. Consider what effect your own state of mind at the moment might be having on your anger reaction. For example, when you're upset or stressed, the fact that your husband never changes the toilet-paper roll and rarely puts the dishes in the dishwasher may make you steam. You see him as selfish, self-absorbed, perfectly willing to leave all the dirty work to you while he goes off to play with the kids. When you're relaxed, you might laugh off the same behavior as absentmindedness or "typically male," or overlook it entirely and focus on what a loving father he is.

Claire, the woman who was convinced that her husband didn't love her, used to become infuriated whenever Doug walked in the door, looked at the mail, played with the children and the dog, and then flipped on the television without giving her more than a perfunctory kiss at best. Simply hearing his key turn in the lock would make her teeth clench as she anticipated the rest of the evening. Claire had reached a point when she didn't care if Doug had had a tough day at the office; she was livid that he seemed so uninterested in her day. Doug, it seems, was truly oblivious to the impact his actions had on his wife and didn't understand why she was always angry with him. His father had followed this end-of-the-day routine, so Doug was, too. Though she'd tried to tell him, he hadn't heard. He assumed that Claire knew he loved her but was simply too tired to show it.

Honestly consider if you, like Claire, might be able to transform your situation if you modified your expectations so you were more accepting of others and tolerant of the ambivalent feelings inherent in every relationship. For the truth is, a critical piece of the anger puzzle is learning to balance the good with the bad, the times you can't live with him against those when you can't live without him. Stephanie, the Bouncer in Chapter 3 who had an affair with another man because she was furious at her domineering husband, realized in hindsight the many times she had seen Stewart in a negative light even when he was trying to be attentive. "I brushed aside the days he did ask what I wanted to do, the times he brought me flowers after an argument. He was trying, but for a long time I was so steamed up that I wouldn't concede an ounce of my anger. That wasn't fair to either of us," she said.

Being able to remember the good is the glue that holds you in a relationship or situation long enough to make changes and find out if it can work. Ask yourself, "What can I reasonably expect from someone else?" Identify whatever you need to do to prevent yourself from sliding into resignation, apathy, or despair when other people don't behave the way you want them to behave: Call a friend, plan a night out, go to the gym—whatever gives you pleasure. Look back at the Safety Measures in Chapter 6 and remind yourself of your expectations and goals. If you can disengage in small ways for even a short time, you free yourself to move ahead instead of allowing anger to keep you stuck.

Remember, as you begin to tune in to and understand your anger, you may also begin to feel sad, worthless, empty, or guilty. But *feeling* as if you want to punch someone in the nose is not the same thing as actually *doing* it—and there's no law against feelings. So don't allow these surfacing emotions to deplete your stamina or throw you off course. If anything, this is a healthy sign that you are finally unmasking the feelings that were long buried by your anger. Once you weather this bumpy patch in the road, they will pass, and you'll be in a position to use your anger as a wellspring of energy and motivation.

PROBLEM SOLVING YOUR WAY OUT OF GRIDLOCK

Effective problem-solving means learning to articulate your feelings in a noncombative, nonaccusatory way so you can have a calm discussion that leads to a new resolution. That sounds easy enough, but most likely you've found that it takes reserves of courage and vigilance to be able to do it consistently without dissolving into childish tactics. When you were two, you didn't have the verbal skills or the emotional awareness to express yourself. If your big sister grabbed your favorite stuffed bunny or took more than her share of the chocolate-chip cookies, you fussed, cried, or screamed in order to express your disappointment and anger. While a temper tantrum might have been age-appropriate then, it isn't anymore. You no longer need to rely on a child's insufficient tools for managing feelings. Instead, by linking your verbal skills to your emotional awareness, you can negotiate to get what you need. It's an emotional challenge, but one that you're ready to master.

The following Driver's Ed rules will help you get to your destination. With them, you'll be able to express your anger safely and defuse any hot situation, no matter how the other person responds. That's what real power, and change, is all about.

LEARN TO HONK YOUR HORN. To break free of gridlock, you must take responsibility for expressing how you feel and what you want clearly and calmly. Take the direct route instead of the back road. Don't assume you know the reasons for someone else's behavior. Many people assume deliberate or malicious intent, putting everyone on the defensive and throwing fuel on a hot fire, when sometimes pure obliviousness is at work. Instead, clarify what you think is going on by asking.

Don't assume that your partner knows what you are wishing, thinking, or feeling either. Use the same skills here. Claire, for example, told herself for years that Doug "should have known" that she needed more romance in and out of the bedroom. She believed that a good husband would know; she didn't realize he had to be told. When she finally started to say it, she was delighted to see that he responded.

Jim, who thought he was no longer in love with his wife, Susan, also learned to honk his horn and assert his need for personal time and space instead of stealing it by lying about where he was and whom he was with. Once he did, he found that Susan was far less demanding. "When she stopped insisting that we do everything together, I didn't feel so much anger toward her anymore," he told me. "I started to enjoy being with her again, doing the things we used to do when we first married. I was blaming her for my unhappiness and expecting her to read my mind." In time, Jim ended his affair with his office colleague and moved back home.

Jim and Susan's case shows that even in close relationships there are times when people are too busy or self-absorbed to notice the effect their actions or words have. To change that, describe your feelings and the impact someone else's behavior has on you. I've found that the format "I feel . . . when you . . ." or "When you . . . then I feel . . ." is a simple but helpful one you can quickly remember even though you may be upset. For example: "I feel irritated [ignored, unimportant] when you don't call and tell me you'll be stuck at the office and coming home late." Avoid the "I feel you are . . ." formula. This simple grammatical shift changes a judgmental opinion, which will inevitably trigger a defensive response or a counterattack, into a statement of feeling.

Problem-solving doesn't give you license to say whatever you want when you want or to pile one hurt on top of another. Unleashing your anger with little regard for another's feelings is not the same as stating your feelings, though many people believe it is. "I feel you're an idiot for doing that" will not convince anyone to see your point of view.

Instead, choose a kinder, gentler approach that shows how much you care and how you truly feel. Shift your objective from punishing to proposing and drop the word "should" from your vocabulary, as in "You should know to clean up after yourself in the bathroom." Better: "would" or "could," as in "Would you please put the wet towels in the dryer after you use them?" Another simple but effective trick is to substitute "recently," "lately," or "sometimes" when you have the urge to say "always," or "never." This worked for Claire. She used to attack Doug by saying, "You never think of me. You only think of your golf game." Now she says, "I'd feel so much more cared-about if you'd spend time with me in addition to pursuing your hobby." By eliminating generalizing, she filtered out the blame.

If speaking up is a long-standing problem for you, practice small acts of assertion. Say something the next time someone cuts in front of you at the bakery line or talks too loudly during a movie. If you're uncomfortable sitting at a back table next to the restaurant's swinging kitchen door, ask the maître d' to find you a nicer table. In time you'll discover that saying what you want is not so hard after all.

STAY ON TRACK. When you do initiate a problem-solving discussion around a specific issue, make sure that it's the only topic you address at the time. Don't dredge up ancient history or get derailed by a laundry list of grievances—yours or theirs. If the person you're trying to communicate with angrily deflects or deprecates your statements or tries to flip the conversation by replying, "Well, what about the time that you...," don't become defensive or apologetic. People tend to get blindsided by things thrown in their path and think they must immediately deal with it. Rather, you need to acknowledge what is being said, but you don't have to address it instantly. Instead, focus on the way the person is speaking to you: "I hear what you're saying"... "I do want to talk about that," and don't lose track of the point you need to make: "But right now I've brought up the way you ignore my desire to go back to work. Let's stick with one thing at a time."

PUT THE GUARD RAILS IN PLACE. Make a commitment to yourself that certain behaviors are simply verboten. Name calling, yelling, cursing, or interrupting means you've both gone way off course and need to hit the brakes and cool down. Sometimes it's not just what a person says but also the tone and body language used that convey a demeaning message. Are you being talked to in a scolding, parental way? Does that look say a thousand words? Then you must say, "I don't like the tone you're taking with me. I don't understand why you're raising your voice, but until you calm down, I think we should table this discussion." In this way you stay in control of the conversation until you are able to move past obstacles in your path.

USE YOUR VERBAL BRAKES to curb your reaction and give yourself, and the other person, time to cool off if a conversation veers toward an argument. The more you try to continue a hot-button dialogue, the hotter it will become—and the more gridlocked you'll be. Remember, too, that initiating conversation about a potentially volatile topic when you're both exhausted, in public, or rushing to get your children and yourselves out the door in the morning isn't a good idea either. And while it's exasperating to have a partner shut down or walk out when you're trying to talk, it's essential that you resist the urge to badger him about the issue once he's asked you to stop or to trail him into another room after he's said, "Enough for now." Using the verbal brakes also means being prepared to take the steps you must when you say, "Let's stop, too." You may need to leave the room or walk outside, to get the space you need for a time-out. This is one of the more difficult steps to take for two reasons: It's hard to tolerate your own anger without resolution. And knowing that someone else is still angry with you leaves you vulnerable. Use this time to reclarify your thoughts. What's more, respecting the other person's limits gives you an opportunity to disengage and learn to live with your angry feelings for a while, instead of feeling that you must do something precipitously simply to get rid of them. Avoid one-upping each other as well, by pushing sensitive buttons and trading accusations that only rev the motor, flood the engine, and cause you both to stall out.

There are many ways to put on the verbal brakes. You can do it the old-fashioned way, by taking one or two deep breaths, inhaling and exhaling slowly as you concentrate on your breathing. You can agree to table a topic for twenty-four hours. Or you can take a detour: Exercise, call a friend, go to a movie—anything that calms you down. Once you feel good about yourself again, you'll be less likely to overreact and better able to stay focused on your goal.

OIL THE ENGINE. Listening empathically and conveying that you understand is one of the most important anti-gridlocking skills. This is when you demonstrate genuine caring and awareness of someone else's emotional experience. When you listen with empathy, you put yourself in someone else's shoes; you feel what that person is feeling. It is the opposite of taking everything personally or trying to prove yourself right. It doesn't mean you have to agree with what the other person is saying, but it does require that you take the time to unravel what is troubling her, or what she believes to be true, and then relate to her feelings.

For most of us, listening is the hard part. It's not easy just to be quiet when someone is talking angrily or accusingly, or has clearly misunderstood you. Most of us feel compelled to interrupt, whether to defend ourselves, to offer an opinion or judgment, or to fix the problem somehow and make it better. Learning to listen without being defensive and negative ("You have no right to feel that way!") and without brushing off or minimizing the other person's perceptions ("How can you say that? After all I've done for you!") is a skill that requires confidence and self-control. But the only way to steer clear of anger traffic jams is to listen for the message behind the angry words. Sidestep your reflex to explain yourself, and let the other person know you care about his feelings, however much he might have misunderstood your actions: "If that's what you think happened, I can see why you'd be so angry. I'm sorry. That's not what I intended." The point is, people won't care to hear your reasons, needs, desires, or goals until you first demonstrate that you care about theirs. Remember, good listening necessitates that you don't bring your issues up now. Wait until later.

OPEN THE HOOD. Bring your anger out into the open and be prepared to let go of it. Learn to accept an apology. Unless you do, you'll stay trapped in the past and obliterate your chance of moving forward. Unload the glaring glances, silent treatment, mind reading, and dropped hints. Use your words instead. If someone asks, "What's wrong? Are you upset?" don't deny that something is bothering you when it obviously is.

As I mentioned earlier in this chapter, to make anger work for you, you must be genuinely willing to give up old hurts as well as acknowledge and support the small changes the other person is making. In my experience, most couples fight about the same few issues, over and over again. If they followed the Driver's Ed rules, they'd zero in on where the anger was coming from, identify the patterns that are leading them down a one-way street, and turn themselves around. "Well, he's supposed to take my feelings into account," snapped Donna, the Staller. "He should have been doing that for the past five years." Instead, recognize what your partner is doing differently today, tomorrow, next month—even if his actions don't meet your very high standards. Don't take the stubborn stance that he should have been doing this all along. He may well slip back into old, neglectful ways, thinking, "Why bother to try? It won't make a difference anyway." Even though you may have spoken up and asserted your needs, you will have thrown a monkey wrench into your own engine. You'll continue to feel deprived and stuck.

To give up an old grudge, honestly ask yourself what's important to you right now. What price are you paying for your continued anger and resentment? Is it worth it? You may be using it to show someone else how much he's hurt you and to try and exact a similar punishment. Discussing your feelings instead of holding that grudge is a much more powerful way to get what you need.

TAKE THE WHEEL and figure out what you can do to steer around people who block your goal. Be clear about what you will do differently, what limits you will set the next time you're gridlocked in the same old rut. People often confuse setting limits with telling another person what to do. Then they feel powerless when the other person doesn't listen or comply. Or they resort to seldom-followed-through threats. In their effort to take the wheel, they become instead backseat drivers, forever puzzled about why they never get to their destination.

To set limits effectively, determine exactly how you will respond the next time you're stuck. Denise, the Office Personalizer, finally told her demanding boss, "Staying late is simply too difficult for me. I'm happy to drive you home after a function, but if I do, we'll need to leave by ten-thirty, not eleven." She also used the Safety Measure of humor: "Well, I suppose I could try something new—going without sleep." Her boss appreciated her levity and respected her comments. By anticipating a problem and speaking up before she became gridlocked, Denise didn't feel trapped and helpless.

ALIGN YOUR OPTIONS AND POSSIBILITIES. Work to build cooperation and harmony by focusing on a team approach. Think in terms of "we" and "us" rather than "me" versus "you." Don't start off a discussion with a declaration of what you do or don't want: "I don't want you to go to the party without me" shuts down all possibility of discussion. It's more effective to state your preference: "I'd rather go together, or skip it entirely." In this way you leave room for an open-ended discussion. Also, ask questions: "What would you like to do?"

Maxine, the System Saboteur in Chapter 4 who had alienated just about everyone on the teaching staff at her school, realized she had to stay focused on the team approach or she'd be isolated personally and professionally. While she used to march into meetings and pit herself against the principal, she now waits and listens to other people's ideas. Instead of telling everyone why she doesn't like a particular plan or textbook, she asks questions: "How do you see this fitting in?"

Reminding herself that they are all there for the same purpose—to help the children—she's worked hard not to take other people's comments personally and to make room for compromise.

If you consistently try to use your anger to bring about change, you should be able to determine over time whether the person or situation gridlocking you is open to change. When things really begin to change for the better, you've harnessed your anger in a purposeful, healthy way. You'll be able to confront your ambivalence with confidence, move out of the should-I-stay-or-should-I-leave rut, while you continue to work for even greater change.

However, you must be prepared for the worst. If you continue to feel that you are driving into a brick wall, your efforts rebuffed and promises repeatedly broken, you may be gridlocked with a person or in a position that can't or won't change. In fact, your efforts to bring about change may be met with ridicule, shame, or humiliation. If that's the case, it's time to learn how to trust your gut and move on. You're in a good spot to do that now; you've already stepped back emotionally, set limits, and put guardrails in place. Most important, you know that you have done everything you could possibly do to give this relationship or situation a chance to work.

DEALING WITH A LOADED DECK:
SPOTTING THE ANGER STYLES AROUND YOU

When you're gridlocked, other people's anger can be as damaging as your own. Below, some of the characters you may meet, and the way they'll try to keep you stuck:

THE TOPPER. Try to confront her and she'll top you each step of the way with what you did that was so much worse.

THE SLICER talks to you in a hostile, cutting way, but she's always "just kidding," and you "never get it."

THE CLUBBER loves to vent her anger actively with abrasive remarks but is secretly afraid of confrontation.

THE TORNADO has a short fuse that ignites quickly and often. You always feel that any minute you'll be blown away.

THE COMPLAINER. Your basic weepy whiner, who never finds anything good to say, or anything good at all.

THE BLAMER always tells you that everything's your fault.

THE POLLYANNA. What, her angry? What are you talking about? Everything is fine. Didn't you hear her? Fine.

THE CRITIC always knows best—and certainly better than you.

CHAPTER EIGHT

TRUSTING YOUR GUT

How to Know When You're Ready to Move On

For Jackie, the Staller we met in Chapter 3, the flash of clarity came early on Memorial Day weekend. As she was preparing the children's breakfast, she casually reminded her husband, Jeff, about the annual barbecue at the beach club. "We're all looking forward to it. It's hard to believe summer's finally here," she said excitedly. "You're not going to work, are you?"

"Yes, I am. You know I have to," came the terse reply. Maybe it was the way he said it, his voice cold and dull—although, in truth, he'd often spoken to her with precisely that lack of warmth and kindness. Or maybe after being tangled for so long in a marriage that made her miserable, she finally understood that she was merely an afterthought in his life. She knew she had to end her marriage, no matter how daunting that step was. Still, while Jackie knew in her gut that she wanted out, she stayed stuck for the next ten years.

Sometimes the moment of epiphany follows the simplest, most insignificant gesture, the briefest look or barely lifted eyebrow. Sometimes, as with Jackie, it comes with words spoken—or those left unsaid. After being unhappy for longer than you ever imagined, you finally understand and acknowledge what you've really known all along.

Trusting your gut is all about recognizing and acting on that jolt of perception before you get stuck—or at least stuck for too long. It's noticing the yellow light before it turns red. Because once you allow your inner voice to speak up—and you listen to it—you begin to break out of gridlock and move confidently toward your destination.

Call it intuition, instinct, or that magical sixth sense, trusting your gut means being able to decide and honor what is truly in your own best interest. Who among us hasn't had that kick-in-the-seat experience when the lightbulb of recognition flicks on and you see, without doubts, regrets, or hesitation, what you need and want to do? Yet while some people are clearly more intuitive than others, it takes many of us years to come to our senses. Almost every person interviewed for this book conceded that, in ways large and small, they "knew" early on that a relationship was unsatisfying or a job situation untenable. Yet they ignored or denied the inner voice that warned of danger ahead and found themselves gridlocked. For some, it took years of unhappiness, even pain, before they experienced that special knowing that allowed them to end their internal debate, break free, and move on.

What took so long? One reason may be that a society so grounded in scientific knowledge simply doesn't trust intuition. If you can't measure, record, and verify intuition, how can you put your faith in it? Although scientists have learned a great deal in the past thirty years about the functioning of the brain, much remains a mystery. However, preliminary research in gender differences does indicate some organic basis for "women's intuition." Women may actually have more neurons in the temporal, or front, lobe of the brain, which governs emotional response, learning, hearing, memory, and intuition. Some researchers contend that women, more than men, may also be better able to juggle logical, rational tasks while simultaneously tapping in to their emotional side.

Nevertheless, whatever intuitive hardwiring we possess at birth can quickly become frayed by years of social conditioning as well as personal history. Intuitive ability is closely linked to confidence and self-awareness. Yet despite a woman's movement that has by now affected two generations, far too many girls still grow up with diminished confidence, their dreams buried under layers of anxiety, guilt, and self-blame, their ability to trust their gut shaken by messages to put other people's needs and happiness ahead of their own. It's not easy to trust your inner voice if all along you've been chastised or criticized for doing so.

What's more, if you were overprotected and rarely had an opportunity to weigh alternatives or learn from your mistakes, you probably don't have a strong inner intuitive sense either. If you were raised in a controlling, authoritarian environment where decisions were always made for you or, contrarily, if you never had enough guidance and desperately sought it, your gut muscle may be weak also. The notions of thinking through a problem, adapting to change, and being flexible in new situations are alien concepts. You may still be afraid to assume self-responsibility because you believe that other people know more than you do. You may still be seeing the world through the eyes of the child, for whom a parent is all-knowing and all-powerful.

You're intuitively challenged as well if you come from a family permeated with secrets, mistrust, or even lies or one where self-disclosure was uncommon and your own questions and perceptions were ignored, brushed aside, or undercut. If you never felt you could trust that others were there for you or believe that what they told you was true, it's not surprising that you are unsure about trusting your own judgment now.

Trusting your gut means first realizing that you *do* have choices—and then summoning the courage to make them, even though you may face a reality that is unpleasant, even harsh. It's a twofold process, beginning with having a hunch that something is right or wrong and then being able to use what you know to make an informed decision to stay or to leave a gridlocking situation. You'll have to be strong enough to cope with the Fear Stoplights—of being alone, of the unknown, of loss, and so on. And you'll need the skills to manage the consequences of your choice. *Don't forget: Staying gridlocked is, in and of itself, a choice to stay stuck and avoid taking the necessary steps that will usher in positive change.*

However, with your Safety Measures in place and your anger at bay, you're ready to make those choices. Even if you're out of practice, even if you've rationalized or minimized feelings for years, you can learn now to listen to your inner voice and tune in to what's really right for you.

SELF-TUNING

To ready yourself to move on, you must shore up your self-esteem and plug any slow leaks. First, give yourself space and time for reflection. Carve out time to stare out the window, jog, walk around the block, or simply flop on your bed and think. Where is your self-esteem sagging? Where, or with whom, are you feeling unhappy, dissatisfied, or unsettled? Write your thoughts and feelings in a journal or diary, and pay attention to your dreams and your daydreams. Do ideas or themes recur? Your gut may be trying to tell you something, so listen up.

For instance, if you're gridlocked in a relationship, think about what you're missing or feel deprived of: attention? compliments? satisfying sex? thoughtfulness? Are you sacrificing what you enjoy or prefer to do in favor of someone else? If you're gridlocked at work, do you wish you had more respect, status, recognition, or money? Give yourself permission to have these yearnings as well as to act on them, regardless of whether others approve of what you decide to do. Remember, it is the hunger for someone else's affirmation—to tell you that your choice is okay, that you are right, or that they understand—that keeps you riddled with self-doubt. So stop waiting for someone else's go-ahead, and *start right now to say yes to yourself.* By affirming your opinions, ideas, and dreams, you bring your internal messages to the surface and begin to reestablish trust in your own judgment. And as you become more self-reliant, you foster the emotional independence necessary for ending gridlock.

Pay attention to external signs of gridlock. I always underscore the importance of tanking up—physically as well as emotionally. You can't break out of gridlock unless you give your body the fuel it needs to run. The latest medical research reports that long-term stress exacts a high physical and emotional toll, leading to coronary disease, a breakdown in the immune system and gastrointestinal functioning, and memory loss, to name but a few—and women, more than men, feel the brunt. Back or neck pain, fatigue, depression, frequent colds, stomach upsets, irritable-bowel syndrome, and other physical ailments are signals that something, somewhere, needs attention, but you're not giving it. Scan your body and ask yourself:

- Are you more accident-prone lately?
- Do you frequently forget or misplace things?
- Are you using drugs or alcohol to deaden your feelings?
- Are you short-tempered and irritable?
- Do you find you just don't have the energy to do the things you used to love?
- Have you lost your creative edge?

Gridlocked people often neglect their health—eating on the run, ignoring low-grade infections, sleeping erratically. One Overdriver who came to see me had been on a series of antibiotics for over a year to clear up a persistent yeast infection. Neither she nor her doctor paid any attention to the fact that she had been living on Diet Coke, candy, and cheese and crackers from the vending machine instead of supplying herself with the nutrients needed for good health.

While you can never eliminate all stress, you can take advantage of proven strategies to reduce it. Making time for yourself to do things you enjoy instead of losing yourself by doing for others is critical. Find something—exercise, meditation, prayer, massage—that works for you, and do it. When you learn to spend time comfortably alone, you fortify your inner security and help combat feelings of helplessness. And anything that boosts your sense of competence and control will ease the physical and emotional fallout of gridlock.

Start slowly, say, with five minutes of quiet time a day, and gradually add more if you so desire until you feel peaceful, safe, and joyful in your solitude. You might also read books or watch movies that are inspirational or even sad—sometimes we need a good cry to help get in touch with deeply buried feelings.

Equalizers, Serial Pleasers, Career Martyrs, and Care Seekers in particular face a Catch-22 when they try to tank up emotionally and unwittingly perpetuate their stuck status. Letting others give to them often makes them feel embarrassed, self-conscious, selfish, awkward, undeserving, or greedy. Rather than take in positive feedback or encouragement, they reject it, which makes them feel even needier and propels them to continue overextending themselves in order to feel good. To break that vicious cycle, they must learn to tolerate those new and uncomfortable feelings and realize that they will pass. Otherwise they will be forever running on empty. So *wait to be asked rather than rushing in prematurely.* Remember, you have a choice about what you do and when you do it. You don't need to operate on automatic pilot. Instead, you can say, "I wish I could help you with that, but right now I'm busy. Can we meet tomorrow?" or "This time I'm afraid I just can't."

On the other hand, some people—like Dan, the Distancer in Chapter 3—have trouble tanking up emotionally because they're too afraid they'll be disappointed or rejected if they do. As long as Dan remained perched atop his macho pedestal, pretending to himself and every woman he dates that he has no problems or needs of his own, he remains lonely. To tank up, he began to share more details about himself—what he liked to do, books that interested him, volunteer projects with which he was involved—instead of always asking questions, offering advice, and rushing to rescue everyone with whom he had a drink or dinner. Although he initially felt self-conscious and anxious, he soon found that when he revealed more of himself, his relationships became less superficial and more dynamic. In time he was better able to tap in to his intuitive sense that a woman would be responsive to him, and he soon broke free of the isolation in which he'd been long gridlocked.

Similarly, Rebecca, the Clinger in Chapter 3 who was gridlocked with her selfish boyfriend, Tim, typically disparaged her inner voice and refused to take in the new information offered by others that might have helped her break out of gridlock sooner. Though she was regarded as one of her firm's toughest litigators, whenever a colleague praised her accomplishments, she either dismissed it ("I know I'm a good lawyer, but so what? I screw up the rest of my life") or distrusted it ("I don't think he really meant it. He only said it because he wants me to help him with his next brief"). Once she started to make a conscious effort to listen to people she trusted as well as to discuss her feelings with them, she looked anew at her work accomplishments as well as at her relationship. She saw the incongruity between how she was acting on the job and how she was behaving at home and began to break free of gridlock.

"The very first night we went out, I knew Tim had problems, and I knew I wouldn't be able to fix them," Rebecca finally admitted. "But the attraction was so strong, and I was so gullible, that I totally ignored my gut feeling."

To fully tank up, you must examine how comfortable you are when others offer advice or support, as well as whether you're good at giving to yourself without feeling anxious and guilty. Start acknowledging your talents so you hold on to the good feelings extended to you by others and realize that you *are* entitled to them. If you're gridlocked, you're involved with people who have a tremendous sense of entitlement about how you should be accommodating them. They are demanding but always unappreciative of what you give, choosing instead to focus on what you don't give. Even more insidious is the fact that their negativity is so pronounced that you often feel they're doing you a favor by allowing you to help them out. You can never do enough for them. Narcissistic, they have no problem thinking about themselves or putting their interests first. In fact, that's all they think about. Unless you develop a healthy sense of entitlement yourself, you'll wind up in the backseat permanently. You have to be willing to feel a little insecure, self-conscious, or uncomfortable when someone gives to you, or you'll shoot yourself in the foot.

Finally, to stay tanked up, you must put any setbacks you encounter into perspective. If a project at work turns out badly, tell yourself, "*It's* a disappointment," not "*I'm* a disappointment." If you regained the twenty pounds you worked so hard to lose, don't say, "I blew it," but rather "I did it once, and I can do it again." Focus on what you do right: "That was a tough group of interns to motivate" rather than "I must have given the most uninspiring lecture of my working career." Instead of thinking, "I'm such a dope! How could I even think I'd be qualified for this job," switch to "Why not me? I'll give it my best shot."

TAILSPINS

Of course, to become more intuitive, not only is it necessary to recognize slow leaks in your emotional and physical energy tank, it's imperative to guard against tailspins—all the confusing, undermining comments and actions of others that puncture your confidence. When you're in a tailspin, you can't act on your instinct; you're too disoriented even to find it. Instead, you wind up invalidating your feelings and desires. Consider the following comments. They're red flags that your ability to trust your intuition is being thrown off course:

> *"You've got it all wrong; I'm doing you a favor."*
>
> *"You're being too sensitive."*
>
> *"You're making a mountain out of a molehill."*
>
> *"I'm not the one with the problem—you're just too threatened."*
>
> *"You're being so selfish; you're never satisfied."*
>
> *"Get a grip."*
>
> *"You're being so irrational!"*

Don't forget the biggest tailspin trigger of all: "You're just too needy." This put-down is a surefire exit door for someone else to escape, leaving you shouldering all the problems.

In hindsight, Rebecca recalled the many times that Tim's flippant comments sent her into a tailspin and caused her to distrust her instincts. "We'd be at dinner with friends, and he'd start an animated conversation with another woman and clearly leave me out of it," she remembered. "He'd literally turn his body away from me, so that I'd have to look over his shoulder or at his back," she noted. "Even my friends would notice that he was being incredibly rude, but he didn't. And he'd vigorously deny it whenever I'd tell him how uncomfortable I was. He was very good at flipping it back on me and telling me I was being my 'usual jealous self.' Now I know that all the times he insisted I was overreacting, he was really excusing his behavior and blaming me."

To fend off tailspins entirely, you must clearly mark your boundaries so you can *stay in your own lane.* People who are gridlocked tell themselves repeatedly, "I deserve more" or "I don't have to take this kind of treatment from anyone." But the question is, Do they really believe it on a gut level? If you do, you have to be willing to behave in a more acknowledging, accepting way toward yourself. When you find yourself in a tailspin triggered by someone's disappointment, disapproval, or anger, you must be strong enough to stay in your own lane and *set limits* for yourself and them as you steer toward your goal. By focusing your analytical skills on yourself and zeroing in on your priorities and interests, you protect yourself from the erroneous judgments and perceptions of others who may have their interests, not yours, in mind.

Consider: Where are you in your life right now? What do you need to get where you want to be? How much interference are you willing to tolerate before you pull out and move on? Remember all the Safety Measures you learned in Chapter 6 that help stem anxiety and guilt and avoid "should" collisions so you strengthen your identity and maintain a clear separation between you and others. If you're gridlocked in a relationship rut, begin to think in terms of "I" rather than "we" by asking yourself, "What do I want from this relationship?" instead of "What does he want?" Then draw the line for whoever is sending you into a tailspin.

For example, you might say, "Look, I want to have more relaxing time with you, but you seem driven to work constantly." Or "Okay, you think I'm being needy and jealous. That's your opinion. It doesn't affect the fact that flirting with other women at a party is inappropriate."

To gain control after a tailspin, remember to *check it out*. Two steps are involved here: self-evaluation first, then assessing the opinions of others. While each decision is yours to make, you don't necessarily have to make it alone. Nor should you simply assume that someone else's perception or opinion is true; run it by someone you trust—a friend, relative, a therapist. Are you overreacting, or are you accurate? Are you jealous, selfish, needy? If the person you trust agrees that you are too needy at times, use this feedback to ask yourself why you may be feeling this way. What steps can you take to become stronger and less dependent on one person? On the other hand, if people you trust validate your inner feeling that your expectations are reasonable, you will gain the support you need to better trust your gut.

Of course, if your past experiences were negative or hurtful, or if you've already been burned by a gridlocking relationship or situation, you may be unable to recognize or even appreciate when you're in one that is healthy. To help you discriminate even further, you need to . . .

TURN ON YOUR LIGHTS

Denial is the hallmark of someone who's intuitively challenged. You forget what was said or what really happened. You forget how bored, trapped, hurt, and anguished you felt. You forget your pain. You're in an emotional eclipse, lying to yourself, pretending that things aren't happening, or keeping yourself so busy that you don't have a chance to think about what's really going on. Deniers minimize the message their gut is telling them ("It's not so bad" . . . "It could be worse") and insist that even if something bad did occur, it certainly won't again. ("He didn't mean it" . . . "Maybe it was really my fault"). Besides, you're probably overreacting ("I'm being a baby. I shouldn't be this sensitive"). In the moment, you vow to put your foot down: "I can't live like this anymore!" or "Something's got to change—and I'll make sure it does!" But the powerful pull of denial washes away all that pain and those good intentions like high tide at the beach.

When denial is active, you experience gridlocking behavior as if for the first time. Despite the fact that someone has treated you poorly time and time again, you remain genuinely shocked and surprised by such actions. You turn a blind eye to the warning signs and see what you want to see, not what really is.

The trouble is, once you get into the habit of denying the crippling effects of gridlock, you destroy the solid information you need to prove to yourself that you can, and must, make a change. Denial may help keep negative feelings at bay temporarily—but it prevents you from accessing them as a positive, mobilizing force.

However, by *creating a "denial document,"* you'll be able to retrieve those angry, hurtful experiences as well as the feelings that surround them and use them to help you get unstuck. Documenting your denial is a powerful anti-gridlocking tool, one that allows you to put shock absorbers in place so you aren't surprised and can actually anticipate and prepare for the upsetting way someone is going to behave. Your denial document will help you recognize the catalog of behaviors that tell you people don't have the ability to make changes on their own without getting outside support—therapy or counseling. In fact, they're only able to give lip service to making changes, without ever doing things differently. In this way, you can hold on to your reality of the behavior you see and finally recognize things for what they are, not for what you wish they were.

To document your denial, write down exactly what happened as well as what was said during and after a painful encounter. Slow down and really concentrate on your feelings. Focus on the nagging doubts that you can't quite put your finger on, so you become clearer about what they really are. Were promises made and broken? Jot down as much detail as you can remember. Do you sense a powerful feeling of rightness and clarity about a particular relationship or life situation? Or do you still feel insecure, anxious, not true to yourself? Sometimes you may become aware of conflicting feelings; flag those, too, as well as the times you minimize what's happening by telling yourself, "Well, it's not that important" ... "I'm being immature" ... "I'm making too much out of this." The simple act of writing these things down makes them real and allows you to refer back to them whenever you sense you're heading into a tailspin. Unless you document and check out a gridlocking comment or situation, you won't be able to retain the concrete information necessary to smash denial and get unstuck.

Don't forget to examine your track record and use your past experiences to evaluate the current situation. Have you misinterpreted the messages from your gut before? Have you often thought you handled a difficult problem at work well, only to discover that you misread your boss's cues? Do you routinely fall for the same type of man— someone who can never commit, who treats you poorly, or who is so needy himself that you have no time or space for yourself? Are you often wounded by other people's actions, only to discover later on that particular incidents had nothing to do with you? Or were your hunches on the money? By understanding how you operated in the past, you can better assess your reactions in the present. If your external and internal markers don't jibe, there's a good chance you're either in or approaching gridlock. Sometimes people's gut feelings stem from the fact that they are unconsciously tuning in to a person who reminds them of someone from their past. Instinctively, they smell trouble. But the hook of familiarity can be sharp. If you can instead learn to trust your hunches, you can steer clear of a bad relationship from the beginning.

Be wary of *blind trust.* I've found that many people who have never had a solid trust foundation have no basis for comparison. Since they've never experienced a healthy relationship, they can't recognize or fully appreciate when they're in one. It's as if all their emotional road signs are in a foreign language, one they never learned. Not surprisingly, their judgment is faulty. So check your emotional road map again to see if your past experiences are sending you in the wrong direction. Take note of any times you've had with loss, abandonment, divorce, or illness that may have taught you to expect only one set of behaviors or attitudes from others. For example, if your parents separated when you were very young, you may never have learned to recognize a partner's uncaring, unresponsive behavior, thinking, "Well, that's just the way married people act." You may sense now that the man you're living with is not there for you emotionally, yet still slip easily into the denial trap and rationalize that since he's paying the rent, the relationship must be a good one. In fact, he may be slowly chipping away at your self-confidence and self-esteem.

Don't ignore your inner voice because you're afraid you'll hear something with which you'd rather not deal. Breaking free of gridlock means you can listen to that voice and still decide—on your own— whether to heed it.

So try on those new feelings and insights. Watch your body's signals: Do you have a knot in your stomach or an ache in your chest when you think about telling a longtime lover to move out? Or do you feel energized and at peace? Is your current position a stepping-stone to a better opportunity or a dead end to boredom? *Once you break through denial, you can tank up with the emotional fuel you need for the rest of your journey.*

THE COURAGE TO PULL OUT . . .
AND MOVE ON

On some level every choice you make or don't make defines who you are. When you choose, you reveal yourself and, at the same time, open yourself to new and different conflicts or problems. But while indecision may initially seem to be a solution, it is, in fact, the problem. Indecision preserves the safety of the status quo and the illusion of limitless possibilities. But as long as you try to achieve certainty, avoid mistakes, and dodge decisions, you wind up in the same place: conflicted about what you want to do, resentful or angry when others decide for you. While the cost of breaking free is high, the price of staying gridlocked is even higher.

Many people approach decision-making from a practical standpoint, drawing up long lists of pros and cons. That's not a bad idea, but I've found it's not enough to be truly effective. For so many people, the cons are simply so daunting and the pros so conflict-inducing that any ambivalence they already feel is inevitably heightened. Before the list is even finished, they're deeper into gridlock. People tend to stack the list in their search for the right or wrong answer, not realizing they have to figure out what feels right. They remain unsure because they are simply not in touch with their feelings. Pro-and-con lists are often based on practical matters and tend to overlook gut feelings. Unless you factor them in, you'll continue to hesitate, waffle, procrastinate, and stall out in indecisiveness.

The better way: Practice getting in touch with your inner feelings on a daily basis by making smaller, less consequential choices. Do you want to eat dinner now or later? Should you stay home this weekend or make plans to visit friends in the country? Say your choices out loud so you can hear how each decision sounds. Imagine following through with it. Do you feel good—or uncomfortable? Can you picture yourself after the choice is made, or is your image blurry? This is not to say that your choice of an evening activity is as paramount as your choice of career. But the psychological and emotional steps you must take in order to make each decision are similar. Each time you make a small decision, you'll find that it feels either right and balanced or wrong and off-kilter. Either way, you gain the self-awareness you need to choose more wisely next time. As you accumulate decision-making experience, you'll feel increasingly better about yourself, free of guilt and anxiety, and more confident to make your own judgments and choices. Ultimately, this self-reliance allows you to step on the gas and pull out of gridlock.

Throughout this book I've highlighted the whys and wherefores of gridlock. Each case history is true—and all of these people tapped their intuition, recognized their stuck status, identified their personal priorities, and became able to make a conscious choice in their own time and their own way. Many years may pass from the time people have a gut feeling that they're gridlocked until they're ready to trust their gut. But once they do, it usually takes only about three to nine months to put Safety Measures in place and actually mobilize for change.

Rebecca's moment of clarity came when she accompanied Tim to the wedding of his college roommate. One of his friends, surprised to see her there, jokingly said, "Great that you're here! Tim always said you were so jealous you'd never come."

"I can't explain it," she recalled later. "For some reason the three years we were together came into sharp focus. Suddenly I saw that all the times he'd put me down and made me feel unimportant, needy, and shrewish, all the times he'd told me I wasn't attractive and couldn't function without him were a charade to hide his own flirtatious, irresponsible behavior and instead make me feel insecure. I'd bent over backward to make him happy because I was too afraid of his anger, too afraid that he'd leave me. And I'd never been left before. I'd always done the leaving. But that night I knew Tim was never going to be the person I thought, or hoped, he'd be. And I wanted him out of my life." As they drove home from the festivities, Rebecca finally told Tim, "Maybe this relationship is working for you, but it's not working for me. I want you to pack your things and move out."

Rebecca put in place several Safety Measures in order to be able to fully trust her gut. She tanked up by taking in compliments from friends and others, which helped her feel less self-conscious, more secure, and less dependent on Tim's approval. By checking out her intuitive feelings with her network of friends and colleagues, Rebecca realized, too, that her needs and expectations were legitimate. She started a denial document to help remember her experiences with, and reactions to, Tim. This enabled her to solidify her inner feeling that the relationship was unbalanced and gave her the confidence to stay in control whenever he tried to throw her into a tailspin and convince her that she was once again being too sensitive. Instead of globalizing, and believing his statements that she was jealous and needy, she legitimized her feelings for herself: "Yes," she reminded herself, "in certain circumstances, when his behavior warrants it, I do get jealous—and that's understandable." But by documenting Tim's hurtful comments and the promises he had made and broken—to seek counseling, to help financially, to pitch in with the housework—she was finally able to zero in on her needs and priorities. "I see a pattern I can predict, and I now know what's going on," she said. "I never held him accountable before. I assumed he'd change, assumed he'd react as I would have reacted. That was never going to happen, though."

Rebecca also changed her CD from one that told her she was a horrible person to one that said instead, "I'm a caring and deserving woman who's entitled to more." Reminding herself that she'd handled painful breakups before and she could do it again, she was able to turn aside Tim's attempts to woo her back. Taking time to exercise regularly helped ease her anxieties and face the fact that she'd been living on rationalizations and denials for a long time. "I have myself back, and I can breathe again. I don't have to prove anything to him anymore—I just have to approve of myself."

After that fateful Memorial Day weekend, Jackie, the Staller, began her denial document and kept track of all the times Jeff treated her disdainfully or threw a long list of "shoulds" in her path. Sooner than she imagined, another collision occurred. When she told Jeff she was thinking about returning to school to renew her teaching certificate, he proceeded to tell her that such a plan was not lucrative and a waste of time. "He also said I was selfish to consider a teaching career, when I could offer to manage his office staff," she reported. By watching out for potholes, Jackie became aware of the emotional hot buttons that her husband often pressed to keep her gridlocked. When Jeff accused her of being selfish and ungrateful, she held her own and didn't slip into a tailspin. She continued to document all the times she felt abandoned, alone, and unsupported, as well as every time she told herself she was living a lie. She then used this journal to keep in touch with her despair, rather than shelving it as she had done for so long. In this way, she didn't forget the painful moments and didn't slip into a self-blaming mode either. When she decided to consult a therapist, she gained additional self-awareness and perspective. "For the first time in years, I feel challenged and alive," she said the day before she asked Jeff to move out. "I really believe that he will never change. He will always try to dictate and edit my life, and as long as I'm married to him, I'll feel like I'll always have to sacrifice my needs to make things easier for him. I won't do that anymore." Jackie finally gave herself permission to do what she needed to do. "I need physical space from him. When Jeff's around, I literally feel smothered in his demands," she asserted. Now she's in the process of organizing her financial papers and filing for divorce. "It's scary, but I know I can handle whatever happens. This feels right for me. I refuse to stay stuck for the rest of my life." That certainty helped alleviate her guilt about leaving.

Danielle, the public-relations Overdriver in the first chapter, realized at a meeting with her boss and client just how unreasonable and unrealistic their demands were. She finally saw that her boss didn't care about her; he was merely placating the client to keep his business with complete disregard for Danielle's well-being. She determined that she was relating to her boss and every colleague much as she had to her demanding and often absent parents, who expected a great deal of their first child. No matter how much she accomplished, Danielle always heard her mother's voice in the back of her mind telling her, "Do more." Since she had always done it all, she continued to feel she had to; delegating responsibility to others, or slowing down herself, was simply out of the question. Finally recognizing that her self-expectations were unrealistic, she started to watch out for potholes on the job when her boss expected too much of her. "He wants me to be unconditionally available to him and every client. He expects me to finish a project plan in such a tight deadline that it's humanly impossible," she admitted. One Saturday afternoon when she was the only one in the office, she sat down at her computer and charted everything she was expected to do and what she was doing to meet those challenges. The list was five pages long, single-spaced.

"When I saw this in black and white, something clicked," she reported. "I realized that at work I consistently give much more than I ever get. Every other part of my life was suffering. That gave me the courage to talk to my boss and tell him that I was no longer going to overprogram my agenda. I devised terms under which I could continue to work there, and I presented him with options and tasks I could reasonably complete. I asked for support from other staffers and told him that I deliver, but that those who work with me don't always come through in the same way. At this point that's not acceptable anymore."

Danielle went on to explain that she could no longer put her name to an account when she knew all along that she'd never be able to meet her client's needs. Though she made several suggestions about changes that could be made, she wasn't surprised when her boss indicated there was nothing he could do. But *he* was surprised when she gave him her resignation letter the next day. "I had saved enough money to give myself a cushion of six months to look for another job," she told me. "Now I intend to take my time—and I have the confidence to do it."

After taking several months off to reclarify her priorities and needs, she was prepared to ask tough questions on job interviews to make sure that the company matched her goals. "In the past I always went for the glamour," she admitted. "I was caught up in the superficial stuff. But look where that got me. Now I realize the most important thing is respect—for me and my work." She recently turned down a job with a well-known fashion-design company because the CEO kept Danielle waiting for half an hour standing outside his office door, never once offering her a seat. She paid attention to the fact that he exhibited flagrant disrespect for her from the start. Even though the position seemed exciting, "My gut told me it was going to be another super-stressful situation." Instead, she continued her job search until she found a company where the people impressed her as much as the work. "I finally realized that the integrity of people, the company morale, the attitude, and the way they treat each other are as important as the type of work I'd actually be doing," Danielle said. "I need to work with people who appreciate and respect each other. People who realize that you can be devoted to your work and still have a life outside." They made it clear that they wanted her on board, and even offered her a salary higher than they'd originally offered. "That validated for me that my initial positive gut feeling was right," she told me. By trusting her intuition, setting limits for herself, and making a long-needed career change, Danielle's successfully broken out of gridlock.

Similarly, Adrienne, the actress in Chapter 5, who was a longtime Care Seeker, ignored the hunch from her first meeting that her manager and agent, Hank, was not looking out for her best interests. "My gut feeling told me that he wasn't going to represent me the way he was saying he would," she reported. "And that's exactly what happened. Hank kept telling me that I was too serious for this part, too glamorous for another one. He insisted he was holding out for a meaty role, worthy of my talents. In one year the only jobs he found for me were either as extras in summer-stock theater companies or one TV commercial." Time and again Adrienne's close friends advised her to sign with another agent, but she felt too indebted to leave. Besides, he kept telling her, "There's a lot of interest in you out there, Adrienne, so don't worry. I've put a lot of projects on hold for you." But each time the promised role never materialized. "It's just a coincidence," he reassured her. "This business is wild. Believe me, if a tenth of these roles come through for you, you'll be begging me to stop booking you." That promise of work kept her gridlocked.

However, when Adrienne discovered that Hank was not only using some of her old contacts to land roles for his other clients but telling people that she was busy and was giving the parts to them so that he could make a larger commission, she confronted him. "I can barely pay my mortgage this month," she told him. "I thought you were supposed to be getting me work!"

"Oh, no, Adrienne," he responded. "A manager doesn't get you work; a manager guides your career. I can't believe you're so unappreciative, after all the time I've put in on your behalf." Adrienne felt as despairing as she'd used to feel when she was younger and her mother denigrated her schoolwork. Since she'd had a history of tolerating unacceptable behaviors, Hank's actions did not at first seem inappropriate. Unsure and afraid of his anger, she backed down once again. But when a plum part she'd auditioned for went to another actress, she called Hank demanding to know what was wrong.

"Okay, I'll be honest with you," Hank said, taking a deep breath. "You're too old. Everyone wants younger actresses." This pronouncement devastated Adrienne and made her feel even more anxious and dependent on Hank—just as he intended. Unable to see through his deception, she began to accept low-paying roles in summer stock.

One night a distressed Adrienne had a long talk with a close friend who reminded her how successful she had been in the past. "Your talent is a constant you can trust," the friend said. "So I took a leap of faith," Adrienne told me. From that point on, she began to document her denial, kept her eyes open for potholes, and avoided "should" collisions whenever Hank insisted he was looking out for her. "Hank kept telling me I didn't appreciate all the things he did for me. I finally told him I was appreciative of the past—but it was no longer enough." What's more, by changing the CD in her head from one that apologized for other people's omissions and worried about all the what-ifs in life, she stopped feeling guilty and started to focus on herself.

Within two months Adrienne signed with another manager, and one month after that she flew to Los Angeles to make a television pilot for the upcoming season.

After many years of frustration and disappointment, Richard, the Bonder, began to see that his longtime friend, Wayne, was simply too wrapped up in his own miseries ever to be responsive to him. Yet Wayne continued to bombard Richard with his problems and calamities, expecting him to bail him out at every crisis point. "The fun, the laughter, the camaraderie simply weren't there anymore," Richard said. "The relationship was an albatross around my neck. I couldn't make it work."

To extricate himself, Richard anticipated the potholes and avoided "should" collisions by altering his expectations of Wayne. Instead of thinking that Wayne would show enthusiasm for his accomplishments, and then being disappointed, Richard began to edit the information he'd always shared with Wayne. In this way he was no longer thrown into a tailspin by Wayne's negativity. He stopped overextending himself by calling to check on Wayne's business, Wayne's health, and Wayne's family. And though he was always gracious when they did speak, he stopped looking backward and accepted the fact that the relationship he wanted no longer existed. Although at times he misses Wayne and the good times they shared, Richard no longer dwells on the past. He's moved out of gridlock and into new and far more rewarding friendships.

ARE YOU READY TO BREAK OUT OF GRIDLOCK?

A self-check list to help you decide if you're ready to pull out:

- You've stopped waiting for permission from someone else to make a move that's critical to you.
- You've stopped trying to get the other person to change in some way before you make your move.
- You are no longer trying to get the other person to understand you. You've stopped telling yourself that if you only tried a little harder, you're sure the other person would "get it."
- You aren't waiting for opportunity to knock; instead, you're reaching out to grab it.
- You've documented how long you've been trying and waiting.
- You've tracked what, if anything, has changed.
- You've identified and worked through your old separation issues with your family of origin, so you're clear about whether and how the past is affecting your current gridlocked situation.
- You recognize that you've shut down physically: You've stopped exercising; you're eating erratically or living on junk food; you can't remember when you had a good night's sleep. You've gained (or lost) a considerable amount of weight. Your energy is depleted, and you no longer feel interested in or excited by activities or people you used to enjoy. You're ready to start taking care of yourself.
- You no longer feel emotionally wobbly, as if you're walking on eggshells in the relationship. You are no longer resigned, anxious, or guilty about the things you do or say.

- You've begun to disengage from the relationship or situation. You no longer share intimate details of your day and no longer overextend yourself.
- You've tried to hold the other person accountable for inappropriate actions. You've tried professional counseling, or even a marriage-encounter group, but the person with whom you're gridlocked keeps insisting that you're at fault.

CONCLUSION

SURVIVING GRIDLOCK

With so many success stories, and so many examples of people grid-locked in love, work, and life who finally tapped the courage and skills necessary to break free, it wasn't easy to select one I felt best represented the points I wanted to make.

Then I met Lindsey, a thirty-year-old hospital administrator, who, when she came to see me, was engaged to marry her longtime boyfriend, Todd, in three weeks. Lindsey's eyes were ringed with dark circles, and she twisted the strap of her handbag as she settled and re-settled herself on the couch in my office. But she looked me right in the eye and, in a soft but steady voice, asked, "How do I know if I'm afraid of marriage—or afraid of marrying this man?"

If anyone was gridlocked, it was Lindsey. She and Todd, a vice pres-ident in sales for a major pharmaceutical company, had been dating for three years. The wedding—a large one—was supposed to have taken place six months before. But when the biggest snowstorm in a century hit the East Coast, closing airports for a day and a half, they decided to postpone their plans until the summer.

As Lindsey juggled her job and rearranged the wedding plans, she'd become increasingly anxious and unsure. "There were things about Todd that always bothered me a little—he can be very demanding and self-centered—but I told myself that no one was perfect and tried to ignore it. But now those things were becoming unbearable. I seemed to have very little patience," she admitted. "I chalked up most of my feelings to pre-wedding jitters. One night I even told Todd I hated him—but my best friend assured me it was common for brides-to-be to feel that way.

But Lindsey felt increasingly distant from Todd. "I hated the fact that he seemed so critical, that he never asked if he could help with the wedding plans. The rare times I asked him to handle something for me, he acted as if it were a huge imposition. He said he loved me, but I didn't feel it because he never showed it. And while our sex life was good, something was missing. I couldn't put my finger on it, so I kept trying to convince myself that I'd always expected too much from everyone and everything, and I was probably doing the same right now. But when I met Michael . . ."

Lindsey paused for a moment, and a smile washed across her face. Not long after the wedding plans had changed, Lindsey joined her younger sister and brother-in-law for a long ski weekend in Vermont. Michael, her brother-in-law's fraternity brother, was there, too. "We just clicked. He's the kind of man you could speak to for a minute and feel as if you've known a lifetime," she said. "He was interesting and interested in me. I kept wishing I weren't engaged, and then I'd feel terribly guilty for even thinking such thoughts." Todd, she told me, is a good man, and she respects him and never wants to hurt him. But she didn't think she could be his wife.

The weekend ended, but her feelings for Michael didn't. For the next few weeks she'd often bump into him back in the city—at the library, the movies, buying the Sunday newspaper. And the next thing she knew, she was falling in love. "The crazy thing is, if it hadn't been for that snowstorm, I'd be married to Todd now. But I don't want a marriage that's a carbon copy of my parents'. They were so unhappy, but they stayed together because of me and my sisters. The trouble is, I don't know how to be sure I'm feeling this way because I'm really in love with Michael—or just scared stiff of being married. Maybe things won't work out with Michael either!"

Lindsey, like so many people I've discussed in this book, was gridlocked because she didn't want to hurt Todd and didn't want to embarrass and disappoint her family and friends. She couldn't make a critical life decision because she felt too responsible for other people's emotional needs and desires, and too out of touch with her own. Confused, unhappy, and stuck, she wasn't able to think clearly and trust her own judgment enough to make the right decision.

With this book you have the opportunity to learn the same skills I taught Lindsey, skills that are necessary to make your own declaration of independence. The responsibility for that seemingly monumental task is in your lap, not elsewhere—which, if you're honest with yourself, is probably where you've long thought it was. But as you've undoubtedly learned the hard way, leaving your happiness in someone else's hands, or to dumb luck or opportunity, renders you helpless, out of control, and dependent—with no choice but to stay precisely where you are.

However, assuming responsibility for yourself, though frightening and initially paralyzing, can make all the difference. Once you do, you're energized, ready to take charge. Finally you see that you have options, choices you can make without being immobilized by fear, anxiety, guilt, or anger. By putting Safety Measures in place—drawing an emotional road map, identifying phantom figures, freeing yourself from old roles—and by trusting your gut, as Lindsey began to do, you find the courage to move out of the rut in which you've been gridlocked.

Lindsey's case illustrates that sometimes the nature of a crisis requires an immediate gridlock-smashing decision. But even if you've been gridlocked for a long time, you have the same opportunity to rally. The Gridlock Questionnaire helps you pinpoint your susceptibility to being stuck. By linking that with a clear vision of the specific rut in which you may be gridlocked and an understanding of the accompanying fear that keeps you there, you gain the self-awareness you need to make a conscious decision to be true to yourself. If you're willing to practice the Driver's Ed skills—steering clear of "should" collisions, staying in your own lane by putting boundaries in place, and learning to honk when it's necessary to assert your own needs, to name just a few—you'll find yourself in control on the road you're traveling, better able to navigate the obstacles that have held you back. The choice is yours to make. Remember you're worth the effort.

By the way, Lindsey and Michael were married last summer.

BIBLIOGRAPHY

Askham, J. Identity and stability within the marriage relationship.

Journal of Marriage and the Family, 1976. 38 (3) August, 535–47.

Bergman, M. Psychoanalytic observations on the capacity to love. *Separation-Individuation Essays in Honor of Margaret Mahler.* New York; International Universities Press. 1971.

Blanck, R. and Blanck, G. *Marriage and Personal Development.* Columbia University Press, New York, 1968.

Bowlby, J. *Attachment and Loss*, Vol. I: Attachment. New York: Basic Books, 1969.

————. *Attachment and Loss*, Vol. II: Separation. New York: Basic Books, 1973.

Dicks, H. *Marital Tensions: Clinical Studies Towards a Psychological Theory of Interaction.* New York: Basic Books, 1967.

Edward, J.; Ruskin, N.; and Turrini, R. *Separation-Individuation*

Theory and Application, New York: Gardner Press, 1981; Second Edition, 1991.

Greer, Jane, with Edward Myers. *Adult Sibling Rivalry: Understanding the Legacy of Childhood*. New York: Crown, 1992.

Greer, Jane, with Margery D. Rosen. *How Could You Do This to Me? Learning to Trust After Betrayal*. New York: Doubleday, 1997.

Katz, B. Separation-individuation and marital therapy. *Psychotherapy: Theory, Research and Practice*. 1981, Vol. 18. #12, 195–203.

Madow, Leo. *Guilt: How to Recognize and Cope with It*. Northvale, N.J.: Jason Aronson, 1988.

Mahler, M. *On Human Symbiosis and the Vicissitudes of Individualism, Annual Progress in Child Psychiatry*. New York: International Universities Press, 1959.

————. Rapprochement sub-phase of the separation-individuation process. *Psychoanalytic Quarterly*, 1972. 41, 487–506.

Mahler, M., and La Perriere, K., Ph.D. Mother-child interaction during separation-individuation. *Psychoanalytic Quarterly*, 1965, 34, 483–98.

Mahler, M.; Pine, F.; and Bergman, A. *The Psychological Birth of the Human Infant, Symbiosis-Individuation*, New York: Basic Books, 1975.

Pine, F., and Furer, M. Studies of the separation-individuation phase: a methodological overview. *Psychoanalytic Study of the Child*, 1963, Vol. 18, 325–42.

Rosegrant, B. Projective identification and separation-individuation in marital interaction. *University Microfilms International*. Ann Arbor, Mich.: 1980.

Wechsler, Harlan. *What's So Bad About Guilt? Learning to Live with It Since We Can't Live Without It*. New York: Simon and Schuster, 1990.

Wexler, J., and Steidl, J. Marriage and the capacity to be alone. *Psychiatry*, Feb. 1978. Vol. 41 (1), 72–82.

Winnicott, D. Transitional objects and transitional phenomena: A Study of the First Not-Me Possession. *The International Journal of Psychoanalysis*, 1953, 34, 89–97.